Mary Berry is known to millions through her fortnightly cookery spot on Thames Television's magazine programme, After Noon Plus. She is a regular contributor to BBC Woman's Hour and often takes part in BBC and local radio phone-in programmes.

Mary Berry was, for some years, cookery editor of *Ideal Home* and is now the *Home and Freezer Digest*'s cookery consultant. She is one of Britain's most popular cookery writers and has written over twenty books.

Also by Mary Berry in Sphere Books:

FAST CAKES
FRUIT FARE
FAST STARTERS, SOUPS AND SALADS

Fast Suppers

MARY BERRY

SPHERE BOOKS LIMITED
London and Sydney

First published in Great Britain by
Judy Piatkus (Publishers) Ltd 1982
Copyright © 1982 by Mary Berry
Published by Sphere Books Ltd 1984
30–32 Gray's Inn Road, London WC1X 8JL

TRADE
MARK

Reproduced, printed and bound in Great Britain by
Hazell Watson & Viney Limited,
Aylesbury, Bucks

Contents

INTRODUCTION

What is supper? To me, it is the evening meal with the family, and sometimes with friends too. More often than not it has to be quick. Husbands have a knack of bringing someone home without notice; children want their friends to stay for supper; people you haven't seen for months appear on the doorstep; or you just feel like having a few neighbours in for a meal and you have no time to devote to elaborate preparation.

Don't despair. It is perfectly possible to produce supper for the most demanding guests in an hour or even less, to enjoy doing it and to increase your reputation as a cook at the same time.

In fact, as more and more wives have full-time jobs outside the home, suppers have become faster and faster to prepare. But they are no less enjoyable for that.

All the recipes in this book are dedicated to speed and simplicity. Most of them are prepared in less than 15 minutes and cooked in under one hour. Many depend largely on the contents of a well-stocked store cupboard and freezer, but fresh ingredients are used whenever possible. The majority are well-loved family recipes that have stood the test of time and innumerable high teas.

Modern methods of packaging, freezing and preserving foodstuffs have revolutionised family catering. But a speedy meal does *not* have to mean instant food. Where packet food appears in a recipe it is used as an addition to the dish rather than as the basis of the dish. For a short-cut to a good sauce, for instance, condensed soups are invaluable – celery, mushroom and tomato in particular. Stock cubes provide a quick flavour for meat and poultry, and packet sauces can be given your individual signature by the addition of herbs and spices. Instant potato is handy if you are really pushed for time and it tastes quite good if you dress it up with butter and lots of freshly ground black pepper.

Don't be afraid to cut corners when you get the chance. You can make a delicious quick pizza if you use a scone dough or even a bought breadmix for the base instead of time-consuming traditional bread dough. Rice or pasta are good filling accompaniments for the main dish – they cook quickly and there are no potatoes to peel. Eggs are perhaps the most versatile and convenient of all quick foods. If you keep plenty of eggs in stock, along with a good supply of cheese, you need never be at a loss for something appetising to offer. And if your store cupboard is well stocked, use your imagination and you need never fear the unexpected guest.

Some useful standbys for the store cupboard are: cans of sweetcorn, beans (baked and kidney), pimentos, tomatoes, asparagus tips, artichoke hearts, tuna, sardines, and condensed soups of various kinds. Also have a supply of tomato purée, stock cubes, Worcestershire sauce, herbs, spices, packet stuffing mixes, chutneys, pickles, rice, pasta, long life milk and eggs. Always keep in the refrigerator some cheese (Cheddar and Parmesan for a start), fats, mayonnaise and a few lemons in a polythene bag.

These are the basics. Other items will suggest themselves to you depending on your personal preferences and your favourite dishes.

Fast suppers come in great variety, that is the beauty of them. You may like to serve one main dish, either meat or fish, with rice and vegetables or a green salad. Or you may choose to serve something very light, such as eggs, fish, vegetables, or a pâté or terrine. On the other hand, you may prefer to add a first course or a pudding, or even both, to the main dish and turn the meal into an event.

Whatever you serve, do keep it simple.

First courses

A first course should be light and appetising and just enough to leave your guests keenly anticipating what is to come. It should not be elaborate to prepare. Simplest of all is pâté, either home-made or bought from the delicatessen on your way home. Decorate it with parsley, fresh salad or fresh asparagus in season, and serve with hot toast. Alternatively, open a can of artichoke hearts and make a simple French dressing to go with them. Serve egg mayonnaise or stuffed eggs, fresh fruit or chilled fruit juice in summer. Make a quick soup from a can or packet, and add your favourite flavourings.

It is a good idea, when you have time to spare, to make your own pâté – liver, ham, kipper, smoked mackerel and so on – and keep a supply in the freezer ready for use.

Fish

Fish is an ideal quick supper dish. Simply grilled fresh trout in butter, fresh herring or mackerel, are delicious and need no addition but a sharp sauce. Buy really fresh fish and cook it on the same day or keep fish in the freezer for up to eight weeks if you are not lucky enough to have a good fishmonger nearby. Smoked haddock is the basis of many marvellous dishes, from kedgeree to omelette Arnold Bennett. Kippers, if you do not care for them grilled, make an excellent pâté and they can be turned into croquettes with the addition of mashed potato.

Mashed potato, in fact, goes particularly well with fish. It tops all sorts of fish pies and fills a variety of fish cakes. Condensed soups can be adapted to make quick sauces.

Meat

Meat is the basis of most main dishes. Fastest, simplest and universally appreciated is the grill – use steak, lamb or pork chops, gammon steaks or bacon rashers. Cook the meat very quickly under a fierce heat and serve at once with a good sauce, vegetables or green salad to taste. If you have time, marinate the meat first to impart tenderness and enhance flavour (you could always leave the meat in the marinade when you go out in the morning).

Meat for grilling should be of the highest quality and consequently it comes from the most expensive cuts. Much more economical are minced meats, sausages and sausage meat. Minced meat can be either from the cheaper cuts of fresh meat or from the remains of the Sunday joint and put through the mincer at home. Use mince for beefburgers, shepherd's pie, rissoles and meat loaf. As a sauce for spaghetti bolognese, a little minced meat can go a very long way. Sausage meat fills pies, patties and sausage rolls.

Offal is ideal for fast suppers. It is inexpensive to buy and quick to cook; liver in particular should never be overcooked.

Good quality lamb is always available and is cheaper than beef. Lamb chops make a quick and easy meal and kebabs and mixed grills are colourful and festive. Lamb takes kindly to a variety of stuffings and to the addition of fruit.

Bacon and ham are invaluable. A little bacon chopped and added to a vegetable dish gives it flavour and interest. Bacon rashers grill quickly and bacon steaks or chops need only the addition of a well-flavoured sauce to make them into a gala dish.

Chicken joints are a godsend to the fast supper cook. All supermarkets stock them – they are packed in convenient portion sizes and need very little preparation when you get them home, just remove the skin and they are ready for cooking. They may be grilled, fried, sautéed, baked or casseroled. The blandness of chicken meat lends itself particularly well to the addition of whatever flavours you like most. Herbs, spices, lemon or curry powder, chicken happily absorbs them all. And for a quick tip, use lemon and thyme or parsley and sage packet stuffing to thicken a sauce and also add flavour.

Turkey, once an exclusively Christmas bird, is becoming more and more popular. New methods of breeding and rearing have ensured a year-round supply of smaller birds more suited to the average family's needs. Most good supermarkets today stock turkey portions which can be used in the same way as chicken joints. Turkey meat is also available boned and rolled in small joints. Like chicken, turkey is the better for plenty of flavouring.

Vegetables

From homely bubble and squeak to delicate soufflés, vegetable dishes range far and wide. Vegetables are an essential ingredient of soups, they play an important part in casseroles and hotpots, they are a valuable complement to meat and fish and they blend happily with eggs and cheese. Cooks welcome them because they help stretch other ingredients and they are quick to cook. They make satisfying and filling hot meals and, served cold, they provide delightful summer suppers.

Above all, they impart their own colour and flavour. Most people enjoy them and even children soon learn that there is more to vegetables than a plate of chips.

Boil potatoes in their skins and peel them afterwards, the improvement in flavour is most rewarding. Baked potatoes, served in their jackets with butter, salt and pepper, cream cheese and chives, make a meal in themselves.

Serve fresh vegetables whenever you can. Buy what is in season and at its best – when there is a glut vegetables are at their cheapest. Serve them as simply as possible and rely on their natural flavours. Green peas straight from the garden with mint and new potatoes go traditionally with lamb – and there is a lot to be said for tradition. A green salad is a refreshing contrast to meat or pasta; crisp celery goes naturally with cheese; asparagus needs only melted butter. These are delights that ask for no elaborate additions. The secret of their success lies in their quality and freshness. And do use fresh herbs when you can.

Frozen, canned or packet vegetables are a marvellous standby for the cook in a hurry. They can be added to soups and sauces, bakes and pies, and used with imagination can only enhance the dish.

Eggs and cheese

Eggs and cheese go together. Eggs and cheese are in good supply in most store cupboards and are an inestimable boon to the cook. Together or separately they are quick and easy to prepare. They make dishes that everyone can enjoy.

An omelctte is the quickest meal of all, you can produce one in five minutes flat. With the addition of cheese or ham, vegetables or cooked fish, or simply a sprinkling of herbs in the egg mixture, an omelette with green salad and fresh bread and butter becomes a truly satisfying meal. And there are sweet omelettes too, with jam, fruit or syrup.

Cheese is a worthy addition to vegetables of all kinds; pasta is practically unthinkable without it. Add cheese to potato cakes, sprinkle it on top of a potato pie before browning it under the grill. Make a Welsh rarebit, try cheese fondue or make wonderful toasted sandwiches

Both eggs and cheese store well. Eggs are best kept in a cool larder or cupboard. Cheese can be kept wrapped in cling film in the refrigerator. Never let yourself run out of either and you need never be at a loss for a quick supper.

Puddings

A simple pudding course rounds off the meal, although it is by no means essential. In fact, the simpler the pudding the better most people like it, and the easier it is for the cook. Fast puddings should be a matter of assembling rather than preparing and cooking.

Only a few of the recipes here are rich and frankly fattening, perfect for a special treat that won't hurt once in a while. Most of them are based on fruit or ice cream. Baked Alaska, for instance, looks most impressive but it is easily prepared and can be finished off while the main course is being cleared away.

Again, don't be afraid of short cuts. Canned custard is excellent in trifle or blended with fresh or canned fruit. An exotic fruit salad can be quickly concocted from cans of such tropical delights as lychees, paw paw, guavas and passion fruit.

Ice cream becomes festive with the addition of fruit or sweet sauces. It is worth while making a selection of these to keep in stock. Fresh fruits fill tarts and flans, and it is easy to stretch a few early raspberries, say, with slices of orange and then serve them well chilled.

After a good meal most people are very happy to finish with fresh fruit. Make sure it is really fresh. Buy it in season, not too much at a time. At their best, fresh strawberries, raspberries, peaches, plums and apricots make a superb ending to the best meal. They need no additions. At other times of the year keep a supply of oranges, bananas and grapes. Dates are welcome too. There is also a great deal to be said for a ripe crisp apple – it goes splendidly with cheese.

If you are serving cheese at the end of the meal, try to offer a selection – two contrasting cheeses should be on the board, with butter and dry biscuits or oatcakes to go with them, and perhaps a bunch of grapes when they are cheap.

The suppers you serve will, it goes without saying, be appropriate to the time of year. A winter night calls for a hot soup to warm the guests coming in from the cold, followed by a substantial main dish accompanied perhaps by rice or pasta. A summer evening in the garden is a different proposition entirely. Slices of cold pâté with salad, chilled fruit drinks, and a light main dish with new peas from the garden or the first of the runner beans can be followed by raspberries or ice cream.

Try to be topical. Use fruit and vegetables when they are in season and so more plentiful and less expensive, and with infinitely better flavour. Keep all fresh food as simple as possible and appreciate its natural flavour. Don't be afraid of instant foods, but use them judiciously and in your own way, as additions to other ingredients.

I hope that these recipes will convince you that quick cooking is fun – and it *is* fun to please your supper guests and send them home feeling satisfied and at peace with the world.

FIRST COURSES

Essentially the first course is light, appetising and refreshing. It should get the supper off to a good start, and arouse interest in but not detract from the main course. Quickest of all first courses is pâté, bought from the delicatessen and served in slices with toast, or fresh crisp French bread, or brown rolls. You can, of course, make your own pâtés and keep them chilled until required.

Fruit is refreshing, either hot or cold – toasted grapefruit perhaps, or chilled orange – and crab meat, prawns and shrimps are always popular. Try combining seafood with fruit in a prawn mango cocktail. Soup is quick and easy if you use a can or packet of soup as a base and make your own additions.

The first course should aim at variety and interesting combinations of flavours. Give your guests something to make them sit up and take notice of what is to come!

American Bacon and Spinach Salad

Wash 2 lb (1 kg) young spinach thoroughly, discarding any stems, tear the spinach into large pieces and place in a large serving bowl. Take the rind off 8 oz (225 g) smoked back bacon and grill on both sides until crispy and then cut into strips or chop finely. Wash 4 oz (100 g) button mushrooms and slice very thinly. Put the bacon and mushrooms on top of the spinach and pour over a little French dressing.

Serves 4

Toasted Gingered Grapefruit

Halve 2 large grapefruit, and separate the segments using a sharp pointed knife or grapefruit knife. Spoon over a little ginger syrup from a jar of stem ginger. Sprinkle with dark brown sugar and then arrange a few slices of stem ginger around the edge of each grapefruit. Brown under a hot grill or warm through in a hot oven.

Serves 4

Shrimp Hills

Core and chop 3 dessert apples and mix with the juice of half a lemon, 4 sticks of celery, chopped, ¼ pint (150 ml) mayonnaise, 2 teaspoons tomato purée and 4 oz (100 g) shelled shrimps. Season to taste. Serve the mixture piled on lettuce leaves on six individual plates, and garnish with a twist of lemon.

Serves 6

Chilled Grapefruit with Grapes

Halve 3 large grapefruit, carefully remove the segments and put them in a bowl. Halve ½ lb (225 g) white grapes. Add the grapes to the grapefruit and mix well. Pile the fruit into the grapefruit shells and sprinkle over 2 oz (50 g) demerara sugar. Chill for several hours before serving.

Serves 6

Crab and Cucumber Cocktail

Cut a half cucumber into quarters, peel and remove all the seeds and then cut the flesh into 1-inch (2.5-cm) matchsticks. Shred 4 lettuce leaves and divide between four glasses. Divide 4 oz (100 g) of prepared crab meat between the glasses. Blend the juice of half a lemon with 6 tablespoons mayonnaise and stir in the cucumber. Spoon the cucumber mixture into the glasses and chill before serving.

Serves 4

Sardine Pâté

Cream 2 oz (50 g) butter with 2 oz (50 g) cream cheese until evenly blended. Drain the oil from a 4½-oz (125-g) can sardines and mash with a fork. Beat the sardines into the creamed mixture, together with 2 tablespoons lemon juice, a little salt and plenty of freshly ground black pepper. Turn the pâté into a small serving dish and garnish with sprigs of watercress.

Serves 4

Avocado and Tomato Salad

Slice 4 tomatoes and arrange each neatly on four individual dishes. Cut 2 avocado pears in half and remove the stones, then peel and slice and place on top of the tomatoes. Spoon a little French dressing over the salad and garnish with chopped chives.

Serves 4

Mango and Prawn Cocktail

Peel and cut a mango into neat cubes and place in a bowl with 4 oz (100 g) peeled prawns and a dash of curry powder, and then add sufficient soured cream to mix well together. Serve in four ramekin dishes with thinly sliced brown bread and butter.

Serves 4

Scallopino

Thoroughly wash 4 small leeks. Slice and cook them in boiling water until just tender. Lightly poach 4 scallops in a little cider or white wine. Make ½ pint (300 ml) cheese sauce (see page 158) and stir in the leeks and scallops. Divide the mixture between four individual ovenproof dishes, making sure that there is one scallop in each dish. Sprinkle the tops with a little extra grated cheese and put them under a hot grill until golden brown and bubbling.

Serves 4

Cream of Celery Soup

Drain a 14-oz (380-g) can celery hearts and purée them in the blender. In a saucepan mix a can of condensed celery soup with ¼ pint (150 ml) milk and the same amount of water and bring to the boil, stirring. Add the puréed celery with plenty of freshly ground black pepper and heat through. When ready to serve, remove the pan from the heat and stir in some single cream. Serve at once.

Serves 4

Watercress and Potato Soup

Thoroughly wash a bunch of watercress and put a few small sprigs on one side for garnish. Remove any coarse stalks and chop the remainder. Melt 1 oz (25 g) butter in a saucepan, add 1 large chopped onion together with the chopped watercress and fry gently for 5 minutes. Stir in 1 pint (600 ml) chicken stock and bring to the boil. Cover the pan and simmer for 30 minutes. Take the pan off the heat and purée the soup in a blender. Return the soup to the saucepan and stir in the contents of a medium-sized packet instant mashed potato and ½ pint (300 ml) milk and bring to the boil. If the soup is a little thick, thin it down with more milk or stock. Taste and check the seasoning. Pour the soup into a tureen and float the small sprigs of watercress on top, or sprinkle with chopped parsley.

Serves 4

Pâté Stuffed Eggs

Slice 6 hard-boiled eggs in half lengthwise and scoop out the yolks into a small bowl. Add 2 oz (50 g) smooth pâté, 1 oz (25 g) butter and a little single cream or top of the milk or mayonnaise and beat well to blend. When the mixture is soft, season well and spoon it back into the egg whites. Sprinkle the stuffed eggs with a little paprika pepper and serve on a bed of lettuce.

Serves 6

Quick Liver Pâté

In a blender place 1 crushed clove of garlic, 6 oz (175 g) smooth liver pâté, 2 oz (50 g) melted butter, 1 level tablespoon chopped parsley, 1 tablespoon lemon juice and plenty of freshly ground black pepper. Blend together until smooth. Turn into a small dish and keep in a cool place until required. Serve with hot toast and butter.

Serves 4

FISH

Fish needs only a short cooking time. Light and easily digested too, it is good for a late meal. Grilled it makes one of the easiest – and one of the most enjoyable – suppers. Fresh trout, herring and mackerel, after a few minutes under the grill need no addition but a good, well-flavoured sauce. For a quick and simple meal try frying herring coated in oatmeal.

Some fish dishes, of course, need more preparation but the cooking time is not long and the results are both filling and appetising. Take fish pie in its many guises, kedgeree, fish pancakes or fish baked in a sauce made from a can of condensed soup, and you have variety enough for a whole season of fish suppers.

Simply Grilled Fresh Fish

Grilling fish is both quick and inexpensive and is suitable for small whole fish such as mackerel, herrings and sardines. The fish should be washed and cleaned and then scored with three diagonal cuts on each side of the body. Season and spread with a little soft butter and grill under a moderate grill, basting and turning once during cooking. Allow about 10 to 15 minutes for the entire cooking time for whole fish, depending on the size and thickness. When the fish is cooked the flesh flakes easily when tested with a knife and will lift off the bone.

Grilling may also be used for cutlets, steaks and fillets of flat fish or cod or haddock. There is no need to slash the flesh, just season and spread with melted or soft butter. Fillets of plaice or sole will only need about 4 to 5 minutes cooking time and no turning. Cod and haddock will need 8 to 10 minutes depending on the thickness, while cutlets and steaks need about the same time as a whole fish and should be turned once during cooking.

Quick Tartar Sauce

Serve this sauce with any plain fried or grilled fish. Any spare sauce may be stored in a screw-topped jar in the refrigerator.

7-oz (200-g) jar mayonnaise
1 level tablespoon chopped gherkins
1 level tablespoon chopped capers
1 level tablespoon chopped parsley

Place all the ingredients together in a bowl and mix thoroughly. Turn into a small serving dish.

Norfolk Fish and Cockle Pie

If time allows use freshly boiled potatoes, creamed. Alternatively, you can use instant potato, as in the recipe below, and adding cheese certainly improves the flavour. There is no need to cook the fish in advance; adding it to the sauce and baking it in the oven is the traditional way. If you have difficulty in getting fresh cockles, leave them out.

Preparation time about 15 minutes
Cooking time about 40 minutes

> 1 lb (450 g) white fish, such as cod or coley, skinned
> 10½-oz (298-g) can condensed celery soup
> 3 tablespoons milk
> 1 level tablespoon chopped parsley
> ¼ pint (150 ml) cooked cockles
> 2 hard-boiled eggs, chopped
> salt
> freshly ground black pepper
> 4½-oz (131-g) packet instant mashed potato
> 2 oz (50 g) Cheddar cheese, grated

Heat the oven to 350°F, 180°C, gas mark 4. Butter a shallow ovenproof dish.

Cut the fish into neat pieces and place in the dish. Blend the soup with the milk and pour over the fish. Bake in the oven for 20 minutes. Remove from the oven and turn up the heat to 400°F, 200°C, gas mark 6.

Using two forks, flake the fish in the soup and remove any bones. Stir in the parsley, cockles and eggs and mix well. Taste and check seasoning.

Make up the potato as directed on the packet and spread or pipe over the fish. Sprinkle with cheese and then return the pie to the oven for a further 20 minutes to heat through.

Serves 4

Kipper Croquettes

If children find kippers on their own a little strong in flavour, you may well find that these croquettes go down well. Serve with buttered peas.

Preparation time about 10 minutes
Cooking time about 5 to 8 minutes

8 oz (225 g) cooked kipper fillets, skinned
8 oz (225 g) mashed potato
1 oz (25 g) butter, melted
1 egg, beaten
1 tablespoon chopped parsley
salt and pepper

Coating
browned breadcrumbs
lard or oil for frying

Put the kipper fillets in a bowl with the potato and beat until smooth. Stir in the butter and half of the egg together with parsley and seasoning to taste.

Divide the mixture into 4 equal portions and shape each into a croquette. Coat in the remaining egg and browned breadcrumbs.

Heat the lard or oil in a frying pan and shallow fry the croquettes for 5 to 8 minutes, turning until golden brown all over. Lift out and drain on kitchen paper. Serve at once.

Serves 4

Fish Cakes

If time is very short you could use instant mashed potato for this recipe, but be sure to make it up using less water than directed on the packet.

Preparation time about 20 minutes
Cooking time about 5 to 8 minutes

1½ lb (675 g) potatoes
butter
7½-oz (212-g) can pink salmon or tuna fish
2 hard-boiled eggs, chopped
1 level tablespoon chopped parsley
salt and pepper
flour
1 egg, beaten
breadcrumbs
fat for frying

Peel the potatoes, quarter them and cook in boiling salted water until tender. Drain thoroughly and mash with a little butter.

Meanwhile, drain the salmon, flake and remove any pieces of black skin and bones.

Add the flaked salmon to the potatoes with the eggs, parsley and seasoning to taste. Mix very thoroughly and then divide the mixture into 8 equal portions and flatten into rounds. Lightly coat each fish cake in flour, beaten egg and breadcrumbs. If time permits chill in the refrigerator before using.

Heat the fat in a frying pan and fry the fish cakes for 5 to 8 minutes, turning once, until golden brown on both sides.

Serves 4

Fish Hot Pot

A simple form of fish pie, served in the dish in which it is cooked so very light on the washing up.

Preparation time about 10 minutes
Cooking time about 30 minutes

10½-oz (298-g) can condensed mushroom soup
½ level teaspoon paprika pepper
1 canned red pepper, sliced
1 lb (450 g) white fish, such as cod or haddock
4 oz (100 g) frozen peas
salt and pepper
1 lb (450 g) cooked potatoes, sliced
a little melted butter

Heat the oven to 375°F, 190°C, gas mark 5.

Put the soup in an ovenproof dish with the paprika and red pepper.

Skin the fish and cut into neat 1-inch (2.5-cm) cubes and stir into the soup together with the peas and seasoning to taste.

Arrange the potatoes neatly on top of the dish and brush with a little melted butter. Bake in the oven for 30 minutes.

Serves 4

Creamy Fish Chowder

A quick main course soup that is quite delicious served with herb bread.

Preparation time about 5 minutes
Cooking time about 25 minutes

 1 oz (25 g) butter
 4 oz (100 g) streaky bacon, chopped
 1 onion, chopped
 2 sticks celery, chopped
 2 carrots, diced small
 3 medium-sized potatoes, diced small
 1½ pints (900 ml) milk
 12 oz (350 g) white fish, such as coley
 ½ oz (12.5 g) cornflour
 salt and pepper
 lemon juice
 chopped parsley

Melt the butter in a large saucepan, add the bacon and vegetables and fry for 5 minutes. Stir in 1 pint (600 ml) milk and bring to the boil, then simmer for 10 minutes.

Remove the skin and any bones from the fish and cut it into small cubes, then add to the soup and cook for 5 minutes.

Blend the cornflour with the remaining milk, stir into the mixture in the saucepan and bring to the boil, stirring. Add plenty of seasoning and lemon juice to taste. Turn into a hot soup tureen, sprinkle with parsley and serve piping hot.

Serves 6

Seafood Vol-au-vents

Make the sauce while the vol-au-vents are cooking. Serve with peas.

Preparation time about 15 minutes
Cooking time about 15 minutes

12 medium-sized vol-au-vents, frozen

Filling
8 oz (225 g) haddock fillet
½ pint (300 ml) milk
1 oz (25 g) butter
1 oz (25 g) flour
¼ level teaspoon paprika pepper
1 teaspoon tomato purée
4 oz (100 g) peeled prawns
salt and pepper
squeeze of lemon juice

Heat the oven to 425°F, 220°C, gas mark 7. Brush the tops of the vol-au-vents with a little egg or milk to glaze and cook them as directed on the packet. Scoop out the insides with a teaspoon and keep the tops.

Prepare the filling: in a large shallow pan poach the haddock in the milk for about 8 minutes until the flesh has turned white and milky looking in appearance and will flake easily. Carefully lift out the fish, remove any skin and bones and flake the flesh. Reserve the milk.

Melt the butter in a small saucepan, stir in the flour and paprika pepper and cook for 1 minute, without colouring. Remove the pan from the heat and gradually stir in the reserved warm milk. Return the pan to the heat and bring to the boil, stirring briskly until the sauce has thickened. Add the tomato purée, prawns, seasoning and the lemon juice. Blend well, taste and check seasoning, adding a little more lemon juice if the sauce needs it.

Divide the filling between the vol-au-vents and place a top on each.

Serves 4 to 6

Herrings in Oatmeal

Very Scottish, choose either 4 large herrings or 8 small ones. Mackerel are equally delicious cooked this way.

Peparation time about 5 minutes
Cooking time about 14 minutes

    4 large herrings
    2 level tablespoons fine oatmeal
    ½ level teaspoon dry mustard
    ½ level teaspoon salt
    1 to 2 oz (25 to 50 g) butter
    lemon wedges and parsley to garnish

Ask your fishmonger to scale, clean and bone the herrings for you.

Mix the oatmeal, mustard and salt together on a plate. Dip each herring into the oat mixture and thoroughly pat onto the fish, shaking off any surplus.

Melt the butter in a frying pan and fry the herrings over a moderate heat for about 7 minutes on each side, until the fish will flake easily when tested with a knife.

Carefully lift out the fish and arrange on a warm serving dish. Decorate with lemon wedges and parsley.

Serves 4

Poached Haddock
with Eggs

As an alternative to haddock use golden cod fillets. Serve with crusty bread and butter.

Preparation time about 2 minutes
Cooking time about 15 minutes

4 large smoked haddock fillets
½ pint (300 ml) milk
½ pint (300 ml) water
4 eggs
butter

Wash and dry the haddock fillets.

Put the milk and water in a large shallow saucepan and bring to simmering point. Add the haddock and poach gently until the flesh will flake easily. Lift out the fish carefully, put on a warm serving dish and keep warm.

Break the eggs into the milk and poach until just set, then lift them out with a slotted spoon and place one egg on top of each fillet. Dot with butter and serve at once.

Serves 4

Haddock Kedgeree

Make sure that the kedgeree is really moist by adding some cream or top of the milk at the end of the cooking. Serve with granary bread and unsalted butter.

Preparation time about 15 minutes
Cooking time about 5 minutes

   6 oz (175 g) long grain rice
   1 lb (450 g) smoked haddock fillet
   3 oz (75 g) butter
   2 hard-boiled eggs, chopped
   2 to 3 tablespoons single cream or top of the milk
   freshly ground black pepper
   2 level tablespoons chopped parsley
   paprika pepper to garnish

Cook the rice in plenty of boiling salted water for 12 to 15 minutes until tender and then drain and rinse thoroughly.

Meanwhile, put the haddock in a saucepan, cover with water and poach gently for about 10 minutes, then drain and skin, remove any bones and flake with a fork.

Melt the butter in a large saucepan, stir in the rice, fish and eggs and heat through gently for about 5 minutes. Add the cream, black pepper and parsley and mix lightly.

Pile onto a warm serving dish and sprinkle with paprika pepper.

Serves 4

Scallop and Fish Pie

Make the topping with freshly boiled potatoes if you have time.

Preparation time about 20 minutes
Cooking time about 30 minutes

> 4 scallops
> 4 frozen cod steaks
> ¾ pint (450 ml) milk
> ¼ pint (150 ml) cider
> 2 oz (50 g) butter
> 2 oz (50 g) flour
> 1 level teaspoon salt
> a little white pepper
> 4½-oz (131-g) packet instant mashed potato
> 2 oz (50 g) Cheddar cheese, grated
> freshly ground black pepper

First prepare and cook the fish: wash the scallops thoroughly and remove any beard and black parts, then place them in a pan with the cod steaks, milk and cider. Simmer gently for 10 minutes until the cod will flake easily with a knife. Strain the milk and cider from the fish and reserve. Cut the scallops in half and flake the cod.

To make the sauce: rinse out the saucepan, melt the butter, stir in the flour and cook for 2 minutes, without colouring. Gradually add the milk and cider and bring to the boil, stirring until the sauce thickens. Add the fish and seasoning and blend well, then taste and adjust seasoning. Turn into a 3-pint (1.7-litre) ovenproof dish.

Heat the oven to 425°F, 220°C, gas mark 7.

For the topping: make up the instant mashed potato as directed on the packet and beat in the cheese and black pepper. Spread the potato over the fish, rough up with a fork and bake in the oven for about 30 minutes until golden brown and hot through.

Serves 4

Salmon and Corn Flan

This flan can be easily made from ingredients that are already in the store cupboard.

Preparation time about 20 minutes
Cooking time about 35 minutes

Pastry
  6 oz (175 g) plain flour
  1½ oz (40 g) lard
  1½ oz (40 g) margarine
  cold water to mix

Filling
  7½-oz (212-g) can red salmon
  milk
  7-oz (198-g) can sweetcorn with peppers
  2 eggs
  salt and pepper

Heat the oven to 400°F, 200°C, gas mark 6.

Put the flour in a bowl, add the fats cut in small pieces and rub in with the fingertips until the mixture resembles fine breadcrumbs, then add about 6 teaspoons cold water and mix to a firm dough. Roll out on a floured surface and line a 9-inch (22.5-cm) deep flan tin. Mark the edge with a fork, line with a piece of greaseproof paper, cover with baking beans and bake blind for 10 minutes.

Meanwhile, drain the liquor from the salmon and make up to ¼ pint (150 ml) with milk. Remove the skin and bones from the salmon and flake. Drain the corn and place in a bowl with the salmon, eggs and milk and plenty of seasoning and mix thoroughly.

Remove the beans and greaseproof paper from the flan and pour in the filling. Bake for 25 minutes until set and golden. Serve warm.

Serves 6

Fried Cod with Tomatoes

It is not necessary to use cod for this recipe – choose any white fish which will cut into convenient-sized portions for frying. Make this recipe in the summer when tomatoes are at their cheapest and most plentiful. Tomatoes are much nicer with their skins removed, and this can be done within the preparation time.

Preparation time about 10 minutes
Cooking time about 9 to 12 minutes

1¼ lb (550 g) cod fillet
8 oz (225 g) tomatoes
a little seasoned flour
2 oz (50 g) butter
1 onion, sliced
1 tablespoon chopped parsley

Cut the fish into 4 convenient-sized serving portions.

Place the tomatoes in a bowl and cover with boiling water. Leave them for a minute, then drain, peel and cut each tomato in quarters.

Dip the fish into a little seasoned flour and pat on evenly. If liked, the flour may be put in a plastic bag and the fish pieces dropped in and tossed until evenly coated.

Melt the butter in a large frying pan, add the fish and onion and fry gently for 6 to 8 minutes, turning the fish once. The cooking times will vary with the thickness of the fish. The flour will give the fish a pale golden appearance and the flesh will be white and flake easily.

Carefully lift out the fish with a slice and place on a warm serving dish. Add the tomatoes to the onions in the pan and cook for 3 to 4 minutes. They should be soft but still hold their shape. Lightly stir in the parsley and seasoning to taste. Spoon the butter and tomatoes over the fish and serve at one.

Serves 4

Macaroni Savoury

This dish is a meal in itself, but for those who are very hungry you could also serve wholemeal bread rolls.

Preparation time about 15 minutes
Cooking time about 5 minutes

6 oz (175 g) quick macaroni
8 oz (227 g) packet frozen peas
7½-oz (212-g) can salmon or tuna fish
4 hard-boiled eggs
1 oz (25 g) butter
1 oz (25 g) flour
¾ pint (450 ml) milk
salt
freshly ground black pepper
1 oz (25 g) packet potato crisps or cornflakes
2 oz (50 g) Cheddar cheese, grated

Cook the macaroni and peas as directed on the packets and drain well.

Meanwhile, drain the salmon or tuna and flake and remove any pieces of black skin. Quarter the eggs, lengthwise.

Melt the butter in a large saucepan, add the flour and cook for 1 minute. Stir in the milk and bring to the boil, stirring, and simmer for 1 minute. Carefully fold in the macaroni, peas, flaked fish and eggs together with plenty of seasoning. Heat through until the mixture is piping hot.

Turn into an ovenproof dish. Crush the crisps or cornflakes and mix with the cheese and sprinkle over the top of the macaroni. Put the dish under a hot grill for about 5 minutes until golden brown and bubbling.

Serves 4

Cod with Asparagus and Mushroom Sauce

If liked, bake a few whole tomatoes alongside the fish for the last 15 minutes of the cooking time. Any white fish could be used for this recipe.

Preparation time about 5 minutes
Cooking time about 25 to 30 minutes

4 portions of cod, use fillets or cutlets as preferred
4 oz (100 g) mushrooms, sliced
10½-oz (298-g) can condensed asparagus soup
quarter soup can of milk
salt and pepper

Heat the oven to 375°F, 190°C, gas mark 5. Butter well a shallow ovenproof dish.

Lay the cod in the dish and scatter the mushrooms over the top.

Blend the soup with the milk and add a little seasoning, and pour it over the fish, making sure that the fish is well covered. Cover the dish with a lid or a piece of foil and bake in the oven for 25 to 30 minutes, until the fish flakes easily when tested with a knife. Fillets of fish will probably take less time to cook than a thicker cutlet.

Serve with sauté potatoes and peas, and whole baked tomatoes.

Serves 4

Devilled Mackerel

This recipe is equally good done with herrings. If you ask your fish-monger he will clean the fish and remove the heads for you.

Preparation time about 10 minutes
Cooking time about 10 to 15 minutes

2 oz (50 g) soft butter
3 level teaspoons dry mustard
2 teaspoons Worcestershire sauce
a little salt and pepper
4 medium-sized mackerel

Cream the butter with the mustard, Worcestershire sauce and a little seasoning.

Clean the mackerel and remove the heads. Wipe the fish dry with kitchen paper. Make three diagonal cuts on each side of the fish.

Heat the grill to moderate and remove the rack.

Place a little of the butter inside the body of each fish and then spread the remaining butter over the fish. Cook under the grill for 10 to 15 minutes, turning once and basting with the melted butter. When cooked, the flesh will flake when tested with a knife.

Place the fish on a warm serving dish and spoon over any butter remaining in the grill pan.

Serves 4

Pasta and Prawn Creole

This dish is a meal in itself, but if you like you could serve it with a crisp green salad, lightly tossed in French dressing.

Preparation time about 8 minutes
Cooking time about 20 minutes

1 medium-sized onion, finely chopped
2 tablespoons oil
3 sticks celery, sliced
1 green pepper, seeded and cut in strips
1 clove garlic, crushed
14-oz (397-g) can peeled tomatoes
½ pint (300 ml) dry cider
1 tablespoon tomato purée
salt
freshly ground black pepper
4 oz (100 g) pasta bows
8 oz (225 g) peeled prawns

Fry the onion in the oil for about 2 minutes, then stir in the celery, green pepper and garlic and fry for a further 5 minutes.

Stir in the can of tomatoes, cider, tomato purée and seasoning and bring to the boil. Add the pasta bows, stir to mix thoroughly and then cover the saucepan with a lid and simmer gently for about 15 minutes.

Remove the lid from the saucepan and stir in the prawns and simmer gently for 5 minutes. Taste and check seasoning and then turn into a warm serving dish.

Serves 4

Goujons of Plaice

This dish may be made with any flat fish that is suitable for cutting into long thin strips.

Preparation time about 10 minutes
Cooking time about 3 minutes

> about 1 lb (450 g) plaice fillets
> 1 egg, beaten
> 3 to 4 oz (75 to 100 g) fresh white breadcrumbs
> deep fat or oil for frying
> lemon wedges

Remove the dark skin from the fillets of plaice and cut into strips, lengthwise, about ½ inch (1.25 cm) thick. Dip the fish in beaten egg and then coat in breadcrumbs. It is easier to do this if the breadcrumbs are put in a plastic bag and the fish just dropped in and tossed in the crumbs.

Heat the fat or oil and then fry the fish strips for about 3 minutes until crisp and golden brown. Lift them out and drain on kitchen paper.

Pile the goujons on a warm serving dish and serve with Tartar sauce (see page 19) and lemon wedges.

Serves 4

Baked Haddock Steaks

One of the quickest fish dishes to prepare, this can also be made with cod steaks. It is nice if served with green peas and sauté potatoes.

Preparation time about 8 minutes
Cooking time about 30 minutes

3 oz (75 g) fresh white breadcrumbs
1 level tablespoon chopped parsley
grated rind and juice of half a lemon
1 egg, beaten
salt
freshly ground black pepper
14-oz (397-g) packet frozen haddock steaks or 4 individual steaks
2 tomatoes
a little butter

Heat the oven to 375°F, 190°C, gas mark 5. Butter a shallow oven-proof dish.

To make the stuffing, put the breadcrumbs, parsley, lemon rind and juice, egg and seasoning in a bowl and mix together very thoroughly.

Lay the haddock steaks in the dish and cover each steak with stuffing. Slice the tomatoes and arrange over the stuffing. Dot with a little butter and bake in the oven for about 30 minutes or until the fish is cooked.

Carefully lift out the fish and place on a warm serving plate.

Serves 4

Plaice with Lemon Butter

This is such a simple way to serve plaice but one of the nicest I know. Small whiting fillets may also be cooked in this way, but they need a slightly longer cooking time.

Preparation time about 5 minutes
Cooking time 6 to 8 minutes

> 4 large or 8 small quarter-cut fillets of plaice
> 2 oz (50 g) butter
> 1 small lemon
> chopped parsley

Heat the grill to medium.

Wash and dry the fish. Remove the rack from the grill pan, put in the butter and place under the grill until melted. Dip the fillets, flesh side down into the butter and then turn over.

Grill the fish, basting frequently until they are lightly brown and cooked through. Carefully lift out and arrange on a serving dish.

Add the lemon juice and parsley to the butter in the pan and return to the grill to heat through until very hot and bubbling. Pour the lemon butter over the fish and serve at once.

Serves 4

Southern Baked Cod

The crispy corn topping goes well with the fish and looks attractive.

Preparation time about 5 minutes
Cooking time about 25 minutes

butter
4 cod steaks

Topping
7-oz (198-g) can sweet corn with peppers
1 level tablespoon chopped parsley
2 oz (50 g) fresh white breadcrumbs
1 small onion, very finely chopped
salt and pepper
4 tomatoes

Heat the oven to 375°F, 190°C, gas mark 5. Butter well a shallow ovenproof dish and lay the cod steaks in it.

Drain the sweetcorn and put in a bowl with the parsley, breadcrumbs, onion and seasoning and mix well. Pile the mixture on top of the cod steaks and dot each with a little butter. Bake in the oven for 15 minutes.

Make a cross in the base of each tomato and place them in the dish with the fish. Return the dish to the oven for a further 10 minutes or until the fish and tomatoes are cooked.

Serve the baked cod in the dish in which it is cooked, with peas and sauté potatoes.

Serves 4

Crab Pancakes

Serve these pancakes with buttered spinach.

Preparation time about 25 minutes
Cooking time about 20 minutes

4 oz (100 g) plain flour
pinch of salt
1 egg
½ pint (300 ml) milk and water mixed
1 tablespoon oil

Filling
1 oz (25 g) butter
1 oz (25 g) flour
a good ¼ pint (150 ml) milk
2 level tablespoons tomato ketchup
6-oz (175-g) can crab meat, flaked, or prepared crab meat
4 oz (100 g) cooked peas
salt and pepper
4 slices processed cheese

Heat the oven to 375°F, 190°C, gas mark 5 and make the pancakes. Put the flour and salt in a bowl, make a well in the centre and add the egg and gradually stir in half the milk and water. Beat until smooth. Stir in remaining liquid and oil. Heat an 8-inch (20-cm) frying pan and add a little oil, pouring off the excess. Spoon 2 tablespoons batter into the pan, and spread evenly. Cook each side for 1 minute until pale brown. Make seven more pancakes with remaining batter.

Melt the butter in a pan, stir in the flour and cook for 1 minute. Blend in the milk and bring to the boil, stirring until thickened. Stir in ketchup, crab meat, peas and seasoning. Spread each pancake with filling, roll up, place in buttered overproof dish and cover with cheese slices. Bake for about 20 minutes until the cheese is golden brown and bubbling.

Serves 4

GRILLS

Grill steaks, chops, gammon, sausages, bacon rashers, kidneys and liver, and you have one of the quickest, and perhaps most popular, suppers of them all. Good cuts of meat are needed for grilling and, if time permits, meat may be marinated first. But it is most important to serve a good sauce along with the grill. A lemon Bearnaise sauce glorifies any steak.

Simply Grilled Fresh Meat

The fastest meat dishes to prepare are grilled steaks or chops, sausages, liver, kidneys and bacon or gammon rashers. The meat should be seasoned and brushed with a little oil or melted butter. On pork chops and gammon rashers it is a good idea to snip the fat at 1-inch (2.5-cm) intervals to prevent curling and shrinking.

If time allows, a very good marinade may be made out of 4 tablespoons oil, 1 small onion, chopped, a little lemon juice and a crushed clove of garlic. Pour the marinade over steaks or lamb chops and leave for several hours before grilling.

Pre-heat the grill to moderate to hot and brush the rack with a little oil or melted butter to stop the meat sticking. Turn the meat once during cooking and baste with the pan juices.

Approximate cooking times:

Steaks about 1-inch (2.5-cm) thick: rare 5 minutes, medium 7 minutes, well done 15 minutes
Lamb: chops about 12 to 15 minutes, cutlets 7 to 10 minutes
Pork: chops about 15 to 20 minutes
Sausages: about 10 to 15 minutes
Gammon rashers: 10 to 15 minutes
Liver about ½-inch (1.25-cm) thick: about 4 to 6 minutes
Kidneys: about 5 to 10 minutes

Quick Lemon Bearnaise

This is an excellent sauce to serve with grills, and very quick and simple to make.

3 egg yolks
2 teaspoons wine vinegar
2 teaspoons lemon juice
4 oz (100 g) unsalted butter
¼ teaspoon salt
pinch white pepper

Put the egg yolks in a blender with the wine vinegar and lemon juice and blend on maximum speed for a few seconds.

Just before serving, bring the butter to boiling point in a saucepan, switch the blender to maximum speed for a few seconds and then slowly pour on the boiling butter. Blend until thick, add seasoning and pour into a warmed sauce boat and serve at once.

Serves 4

PORK

Use the best cuts of pork for grilling and cook them quickly under a fierce heat. Grilled pork is excellent served with a piquant sauce.

One very quick method of cooking is stir frying, and this is a particularly good way to cook pork fillet. The secret of stir frying is to cut the meat into very fine strips which cook very quickly. Vegetables cut in tiny pieces are then added to the pan and the whole colourful dish, including the preparation, is ready to eat in about 15 minutes.

Oriental Pork

This dish is good enough for visitors.

Preparation time about 25 minutes
Cooking time about 20 minutes

1 lb (450 g) lean pork
1 tablespoon oil
1 onion, chopped
¼ pint (150 ml) water
2 tablespoons soy sauce
1 tablespoon vinegar
1 level tablespoon demerara sugar
14½-oz (410-g) can pineapple chunks
1 rounded tablespoon cornflour
salt and pepper
1 cabbage
salt
butter
freshly ground black pepper

Cut the pork into neat thin strips, removing any excess fat. Heat the oil in a frying pan and add the pork and onion and fry for 5 minutes to seal the pork. Stir in the water, soy sauce, vinegar, sugar and the contents of the can of pineapple. Bring to the boil, cover the pan with a lid or piece of foil and simmer for 15 minutes.

Blend the cornflour with a little cold water and stir into the sauce, then bring to the boil, stirring until thickened. Season to taste.

Meanwhile, very finely shred the cabbage and put it in a large saucepan with the salt, 3 tablespoons water and a large knob of butter and cook over a moderate heat for about 5 minutes, shaking the pan frequently. Drain any liquor into the pork and then season the cabbage with plenty of black pepper. Arrange the cabbage around the edge of a warm serving dish and spoon the pork into the centre.

Serves 4

Stir Fry Pork

This recipe can also be made using prawns or chicken breast cut in thin strips. Serve with plain boiled rice.

Preparation time about 5 minutes
Cooking time about 8 to 10 minutes

12 oz (350 g) pork fillet
8 oz (225 g) white cabbage
3 spring onions
2 level teaspoons cornflour
2 tablespoons sherry
2 tablespoons corn oil
salt
ground black pepper
8 oz (225 g) bean sprouts
1 clove garlic, crushed
¼ pint (150 ml) stock
2 tablespoons soy sauce

Cut the pork into fine pencil strips about 2 inches (5 cm) long. Shred the cabbage very finely and cut the spring onions into short lengths. Blend the cornflour with the sherry.

Heat the oil in a wok or large heavy pan until very hot. Season the pork and then add to the pan and cook over a fierce heat, tossing and moving it all the time for 1 minute. Lift out with a slotted spoon and put on a plate.

Reheat the wok or pan and add the cabbage, spring onions, bean sprouts and garlic. Cook for a few minutes, tossing all the time, then return the pork to the pan and stir in the stock and soy sauce and blended cornflour. Cook for at least another minute or until the liquid is creamy and the vegetables still crisp. Taste and check seasoning.

Serves 4

Stuffed Pork Chops

Sage and onion stuffing is a natural with pork. Remove the rind from the chops before grilling, and carefully slash the skin with a sharp knife. Grill the rind with the chops and serve as crackling.

Preparation time about 10 minutes
Cooking time about 16 minutes

4 pork chops
4 level tablespoons packet sage and onion stuffing mix
4 tomatoes
watercress

Prepare a medium grill and remove the grill rack.

Remove the rind from the chops and reserve. Make a horizontal cut through the centre of each chop to the bone to make a large pocket. Make up the stuffing as directed on the packet and fill the pockets and then press back into shape.

Place the chops in the grill pan with the crackling and grill for about 8 minutes. Turn the chops over and add the whole tomatoes, with just a cross cut on top, and grill for a further 8 minutes until the pork is tender and the juices run clear.

Arrange the chops on a serving dish with the tomatoes and crackling and garnish with watercress.

Serves 4

Churchill Pork

A very simple, very special pork dish which is nice served with buttered noodles.

Preparation time about 20 minutes
Cooking time about 15 minutes

  2 tablespoons oil
  1 oz (25 g) butter
  a large pork fillet cut in ½ inch (1.25 cm) slices
  1 very large onion, sliced
  1 oz (25 g) flour
  generous ½ pint (300 ml) water
  1 chicken stock cube
  2 tablespoons tomato purée
  1 tablespoon redcurrant jelly
  2 tablespoons sherry
  6 oz (175 g) mushrooms, sliced
  ¼ pint (150 ml) soured cream
  salt and pepper
  chopped parsley

Heat the oil and butter in a large shallow pan and brown the pork slices over a high heat, turning them as each side browns. Lift out the meat with a slotted spoon and put on a plate on one side.

Add the onion to the pan and cook gently, stirring until a pale golden colour. Stir in the flour and cook for a few moments. Add the water, stock cube, purée, jelly and sherry and bring to the boil, stirring.

Return the pork to the pan with the mushrooms, season well and cook gently for 15 minutes. Remove the pan from the heat, taste and adjust seasoning.

Just before serving, stir in the soured cream. Turn into a warm dish and sprinkle with chopped parsley.

Serves 4

Pork Chops in Orange Sauce

This is a different way to serve pork chops and the delicious sauce makes the dish good enough for informal entertaining.

Preparation time about 15 minutes
Cooking time about 20 to 25 minutes

  1 orange
  1 oz (25 g) dripping
  4 pork chops, rinded
  1 large onion, sliced
  1 oz (25 g) flour
  ½ pint (300 ml) chicken stock
  salt and pepper

Thinly peel the rind from the orange. Cut the rind into thin strips with a sharp knife, place them in a small pan, cover with cold water and bring to the boil. Drain. Squeeze the juice from the orange.

Melt the dripping in a frying pan and fry the pork chops with the onions until golden brown on both sides, then lift out and put on a plate.

Stir the flour into the fat in the pan and cook for 1 minute. Add the stock and bring to the boil, stirring. Add the orange juice and rind and return the chops and onions to the pan. Season well, cover the pan and simmer for about 20 minutes or until the chops are tender. The time will vary a little depending on the thickness of the chops.

Serve with creamy mashed potato.

Serves 4

Pork Ring with Barbecued Baked Beans

Serve this with chunks of French bread to soak up the spare sauce. Dutch pork rings usually come in vacuum packs and are boiled in the bag for about 15 minutes. Slices of pork sausage also go well with a good thick soup.

Making time 15 minutes

8½ oz (240 g) smoked pork sausage
2 tablespoons oil
2 onions, chopped
2 sticks celery, sliced
1 green pepper, seeded and chopped
2 × 15½-oz (439-g) cans baked beans in tomato sauce
3 oz (75 g) dark soft brown sugar
1 to 2 tablespoons Worcestershire sauce
a little freshly ground black pepper
1 level teaspoon French mustard
3 tablespoons tomato ketchup

Cook the sausage as directed on the packet.

Meanwhile, heat the oil in a saucepan, add the onion, celery and green pepper, cover and cook for 10 minutes or until soft. Then add the remaining ingredients to the pan. Heat them through, and then simmer for about 5 minutes.

Remove the sausage from the bag and cut it into slices. Stir the sausage slices into the bean mixture and heat through. Taste and check seasoning and pour into a warm serving dish or casserole.

Serves 4 to 6

Cowboys Pork and Beans

Pork and Beans is very popular with the young, especially if they have spent the afternoon playing Cowboys and Indians. Serve it just as it is with large chunks of home-made bread or rolls.

Preparation time about 12 minutes
Cooking time about 30 to 40 minutes

1 oz (25 g) pork dripping
1 onion, chopped
3 sticks celery, sliced
1 lb (450 g) belly pork, sliced
15½-oz (439-g) can baked beans in tomato sauce
1 tablespoon Worcestershire sauce
1 level teaspoon made mustard
salt and pepper

Melt the dripping in a saucepan and fry the onion and celery for 5 minutes.

Remove the rind and any bone from the pork slices and cut across into strips.

Add the pork and all the remaining ingredients to the saucepan and bring to the boil, stirring. Reduce the heat, cover with a tight fitting lid and simmer for about 30 to 40 minutes or until the pork is tender.

Taste and check seasoning. Turn into a warm serving dish.

Serves 4

Piquant Pork

This slightly spicy pork and rice dish is an excellent way to use up the last of the Sunday joint.

Making time about 20 minutes

8 oz (225 g) long grain rice
1 oz (25 g) pork dripping
2 onions, sliced
8-oz (227-g) packet frozen mixed vegetables
4 tablespoons soy sauce
1 level teaspoon curry powder
salt
freshly ground black pepper
about 8 oz (225 g) cooked pork, diced

Cook the rice in fast-boiling salted water until tender, as directed on the packet. Drain and rinse well.

Meanwhile, melt the dripping in a large saucepan, add the onions and fry quickly until soft and a pale golden brown.

Cook the mixed vegetables as directed on the packet, and then stir into the pan with the rice, soy sauce, curry powder, salt and pepper and cooked pork.

Heat through, stirring continuously, until the ingredients are well mixed and piping hot. Taste and check seasoning. Turn into a warm casserole or serving dish.

Serves 4

Spanish Pork

Serve this recipe with plain boiled noodles or rice to soak up the tomato and pepper sauce.

Preparation time about 10 minutes
Cooking time about 30 minutes

4 spare rib pork chops
a little seasoned flour
1 tablespoon oil
1 onion, sliced
1 green pepper, seeded and sliced
14-oz (397-g) can peeled tomatoes
salt
freshly ground black pepper
¼ pint (150 ml) chicken stock

Remove any rind from the chops and coat each chop in flour.

Heat the oil in a frying pan and fry the chops with the onion until lightly browned on each side. Add the remaining ingredients to the pan and bring to the boil. Cover the pan, then reduce the heat and simmer gently for about 30 minutes or until the pork is tender. The cooking time will vary a little according to the thickness of the chops.

Taste the sauce and check seasoning.

Lift the chops out of the pan and arrange on a serving dish. Spoon the sauce over and around the meat.

Serves 4

Oaty Pork Burgers

This is a tasty way to serve the last of the joint, and the addition of apple makes the burgers nice and moist. If time is short, chop the onion and meat finely instead of mincing it.

Preparation time about 10 minutes
Cooking time about 6 to 8 minutes

> about 8 to 10 oz (225 to 275 g) cooked pork
> 1 small onion
> 1 medium-sized cooking apple, peeled, cored and quartered
> 4 oz (100 g) fresh white or brown breadcrumbs
> ½ level teaspoon dried sage
> salt and pepper
> 1 egg, beaten to mix
> a little flour
> beaten egg, to coat
> rolled oats
> pork dripping

Remove any skin and excess fat from the pork and mince it with the onion and apple into a bowl. Add the breadcrumbs, sage, seasoning and 1 egg and mix well to form a firm mixture.

With lightly floured hands, shape the mixture into 8 burgers. Coat the burgers in beaten egg and roll them in the oats.

Heat the dripping in a frying pan and fry the burgers for 3 to 4 minutes on each side until crisp and golden brown. Serve with a good tomato sauce.

Serves 4

Crispy Orange Chops

This dish is good enough for an informal supper party. Serve the chops with sauté potatoes and a green vegetable such as broccoli spears.

Preparation time about 10 minutes
Cooking time about 15 minutes

   1 orange
   1 rounded tablespoon demerara sugar
   1 level tablespoon honey
   1 level teaspoon dry mustard
   1 teaspoon Worcestershire sauce
   4 pork chops
   3 oz (75 g) fresh white breadcrumbs
   a little fat for frying

Cut 4 thin slices from the orange and make a small cut into the centre of each slice. Grate the rind and squeeze the juice from the remaining part of the orange. Place the orange rind in a small bowl with 1 tablespoon of the orange juice, the sugar, honey, mustard and Worcestershire sauce. Mix well.

Remove the rind from the pork chops and trim off any excess fat. Spread the orange mixture over each chop and coat in the breadcrumbs, patting the crumbs on firmly so that the chops are completely covered.

Heat a little fat in a frying pan and fry the chops for about 15 minutes, turning once so that they are golden brown and crisp on the outside and cooked inside.

Lift the chops out of the frying pan and place on a warm serving dish. Garnish each chop with a twisted slice of orange, and a sprig of watercress if liked.

Serves 4

LAMB

Lamb cutlets are the foundation of a quick mixed grill. Lamb chops can be grilled and served with mint sauce, and good lean lamb makes the ever-popular kebabs. To make kebabs, marinate the meat in advance if you can and cook it very fast.

Special Lamb Grill

A mixed grill is always popular. Serve with sauté potatoes and a green salad or green peas.

Preparation time about 15 minutes
Cooking time about 10 to 12 minutes

2 oz (50 g) butter
1 level tablespoon chopped parsley
a little lemon juice
freshly ground black pepper
4 lamb cutlets
4 lambs' kidneys
4 rashers back bacon
4 tomatoes
4 large flat mushrooms

Put the butter in a small bowl with the parsley, lemon juice and black pepper and cream together until thoroughly mixed. Place the butter on a piece of foil and shape into a roll, and then chill well.

Trim the cutlets if necessary. Remove any fat and skin from the kidneys, snip out the core with a pair of scissors or a sharp pointed knife and leave them whole. Cut the rind from the bacon and roll up the rashers. Mark a cross on the top of each tomato. Trim the stalks from the mushrooms.

Heat the grill to moderate to hot and remove the rack. Place the cutlets, and kidneys in the grill pan and cook for 2 minutes, then add the bacon and tomatoes and continue cooking for a further 5 minutes. Turn over the cutlets, kidneys and bacon and add the mushrooms to the pan, and grill for a further 5 minutes or until cooked.

Lift the ingredients out of the grill pan and arrange on a serving dish. Remove the butter roll from the refrigerator and cut into 8 slices. Place 2 slices on each cutlet and serve at once.

Serves 4

Lamb and Tomato Packets

Cooking in foil makes the lamb beautifully moist and tender. It also gives it a lovely flavour.

Preparation time about 10 minutes
Cooking time about 30 minutes

4 lamb chump chops
½ oz (12.5 g) flour
½ oz (12.5 g) dripping
1 large onion, chopped
1 clove garlic, crushed
12 oz (350 g) tomatoes, skinned and quartered
¼ level teaspoon mixed dried herbs
salt
freshly ground black pepper

Heat the oven to 375°F, 190°C, gas mark 5.

Trim any excess fat from the chops and coat in flour. Heat the dripping in a frying pan and quickly fry the chops until golden brown on both sides. Lift out and place each chop on a 10-inch (25-cm) square of foil.

Add the onion and garlic to the pan and fry for 5 minutes. Stir in the tomatoes, herbs and seasoning, mix well and cook for 1 minute. Divide the tomato mixture between each chop, seal the foil and bake in the oven for 30 minutes.

Serve with creamy mashed potato to soak up the juices.

Serves 4

Mint Glazed Lamb Chops

A very fast supper dish. While the chops are grilling, cook some peas and small new potatoes to go with the lamb.

Preparation time about 2 minutes
Cooking time about 16 to 20 minutes

> *4 lamb chops, seasoned*
> *mint jelly*
> *4 tomatoes, halved*
> *sprigs of watercress to garnish*

Heat the grill to moderate and remove the rack from the pan.

Lay the chops in the grill pan and spread each with 1 heaped teaspoon of mint jelly. Place the chops under the grill and cook for about 8 to 10 minutes. The time will vary according to the thickness of the chops.

Turn the chops over and spread each one with 1 further teaspoon of mint jelly. Add the tomatoes to the grill pan and then return it to the grill and continue cooking for a further 8 to 10 minutes until the lamb is tender and the chops are glazed.

Arrange the chops and the tomatoes on a warm serving dish. Garnish with sprigs of watercress.

Serves 4

Lamb Kebabs

It is important to use good lean lamb for kebabs because of the fast cooking time. If you ask your butcher he will probably be able to find you a neck fillet, which is ideal. Prepare the marinade and the meat early in the day, then all you need to do is to pop the meat and vegetables on skewers and turn on the grill.

Preparation time about 10 minutes
Cooking time about 10 minutes

1 lb (450 g) neck fillet or leg of lamb
4 tomatoes, halved
16 button mushrooms
bay leaves
salt and pepper

Marinade
2 tablespoons oil
1 tablespoon wine vinegar
1 clove garlic, crushed
salt
freshly ground black pepper

Cut the lamb into neat 1-inch (2.5-cm) cubes. Blend all the marinade ingredients together and pour over the meat in a bowl. Cover and leave to marinate for about 8 hours.

Heat the grill to hot.

Oil four long skewers and alternately thread on the lamb, tomatoes, mushrooms and bay leaves. Season lightly and then put under the grill and grill for about 10 minutes, turning frequently until the lamb is tender.

Put the kebabs on a warm dish and serve with rice and a crisp green salad.

Serves 4

Crispy Cutlets with Tomato Rice

This is a different way to serve cutlets that makes them deliciously crisp. It is not at all difficult to do. For a change, you could use a can of condensed mushroom soup.

Preparation time about 15 minutes
Cooking time about 8 to 10 minutes

6 oz (175 g) long grain rice
8 small lamb cutlets or 4 large chops
1 egg, beaten
browned breadcrumbs
about 2 oz (50 g) lard
4 oz (100 g) garden peas, cooked
10½-oz (298-g) can condensed tomato soup
salt and pepper

Cook the rice as directed on the packet in plenty of fast boiling salted water. Drain.

Trim any excess fat from the cutlets. Put the egg in a shallow dish and the breadcrumbs in a plastic bag. First dip the cutlets in the beaten egg and then coat in the breadcrumbs by tossing them in the bag. Pat the crumbs on firmly and shake off any surplus.

Heat the lard in a frying pan and fry the cutlets on each side for about 4 to 5 minutes. The length of time will vary a little with the thickness of the cutlets. Lift out and drain on kitchen paper.

Rinse out the saucepan in which the rice was cooked and return the rice to it, together with the peas and soup. Heat the mixture through, stirring until thoroughly mixed. Taste and add seasoning if necessary.

Pile the rice onto a warm serving dish and then arrange the cutlets on top.

Serves 4

Curzon Lamb Grill

This is a good variation on the basic grilled lamb chop theme. The apple and lemon in the topping give the lamb a sharp flavour.

Preparation time about 5 minutes
Cooking time about 20 minutes

4 lamb chump chops
oil

Topping
1 small cooking apple
1 level teaspoon grated lemon rind
4 level tablespoons parsley and thyme stuffing mix
4 tablespoons boiling water

Heat the grill to moderate.

Place the chops on the grill rack and brush them with a little oil. Cook under the grill for about 15 minutes, turning once until the chops are golden brown and tender.

Meanwhile, peel, core and coarsely grate the apple into a bowl. Add the other topping ingredients and mix thoroughly.

When the chops are cooked, divide the topping between them and spoon over the juices from the grill pan. Return to the grill for a further 5 minutes to allow the stuffing to get hot through and turn a golden brown on top.

Lift the chops onto a warm serving dish and serve with green beans, sauté potatoes and, if liked, halved grilled tomatoes which may be cooked under the grill with the chops for 5 to 10 minutes.

Serves 4

Lamb Espagnole

Lamb chops go very well with a rich tomato sauce like the one given here, and noodles make a good base for the dish.

Preparation time about 10 minutes
Cooking time about 20 minutes

8 oz (225 g) egg noodles
1 oz (25 g) butter
freshly ground black pepper
4 lamb chops
salt and pepper

Sauce
1 carrot, chopped
1 onion, chopped
1 tablespoon oil
1 oz (25 g) flour
19-fl oz (540-ml) can tomato juice
½ level teaspoon dried marjoram
salt and pepper

To make the sauce, cook the carrot and onion in the oil for 5 minutes, and then stir in the flour and cook for 1 minute. Blend in the tomato juice, herbs and seasoning and bring to the boil, stirring. Reduce the heat and simmer for 20 minutes.

Meanwhile, cook the noodles in plenty of fast boiling salted water as directed on the packet. Drain well and then return noodles to the pan with the butter. Toss well and add plenty of black pepper.

Heat the grill to hot. Season the chops and grill for about 15 minutes, turning once. Place the noodles on a warm serving dish and lay the chops on top. Stir any juices left in the grill pan into the sauce. Taste and check seasoning and then spoon over the chops. Serve at once.

Serves 4

Ortago Lamb

This recipe calls for shoulder cuts of lamb – also known as shoulder chops, blade chops or shoulder slices. They are lean and meaty.

Preparation time about 10 minutes
Cooking time about 45 minutes

> 4 lamb shoulder cuts
> salt
> freshly ground black pepper
> 1 tablespoon oil
> 1 level tablespoon flour
> 1 level teaspoon cinnamon
> ½ pint (300 ml) stock
> 8-oz (227-g) can apricot halves

Season the chops. Heat the oil in a large shallow pan, then add the chops and brown on both sides. Lift out the chops onto a plate.

Stir the flour and cinnamon into the fat remaining in the pan and then blend in the stock, stirring continuously. Add the apricots and the juice. Return the lamb to the pan, cover with a lid and simmer very gently for about 45 minutes or until the lamb is tender. Taste and check seasoning.

Serve with creamed potatoes and buttered leeks.

Serves 4

North Auckland Lamb

This makes a delicious, inexpensive roast for two to three people.

Preparation time about 2 to 3 minutes
Cooking time about 1¼ hours

½ shoulder of lamb, knuckle end
1 clove garlic, crushed
1 tablespoon flour, seasoned
1 large cooking apple, peeled, cored and chopped
7-oz (198-g) can pineapple pieces or cubes
1 tablespoon sultanas
¼ pint (150 ml) water
1 chicken stock cube, crumbled

Heat the oven to 350°F, 180°C, gas mark 4.

Rub the shoulder of lamb with garlic and flour and put all the other ingredients in the roasting tin, including the pineapple juice. Place the lamb on top and roast for about 1¼ hours basting with the juices during cooking.

Lift out the joint and place on a warm serving dish.

Taste the juices to check seasoning. If the apple was sour, a dash of sugar will improve the gravy. Turn into a gravy boat and serve with the lamb.

Serves 2 to 3

MINCED BEEF

Minced beef is, above all, versatile. It is economical too, and a little can go a long way. Mince is quickly prepared, quickly cooked and universally popular whether it is used as the basis of meat balls, an economical spaghetti sauce or an exotic chilli con carne (perfect for impressing friends at an impromptu supper party).

American Meat Balls

Adding stuffing mix to the meat balls means that there are no bread-crumbs to make. They also taste beautifully herby and hold together well. Serve them with noodles.

Preparation time about 15 minutes
Cooking time about 20 minutes

1 lb (450 g) minced beef
2 oz (50 g) parsley and thyme stuffing mix
1 egg
salt
freshly ground black pepper
flour
1 oz (25 g) dripping
1½-pint (900-ml) packet minestrone soup mix
¾ pint (450 ml) water

Place the the mince in a bowl with the stuffing mix, egg and seasoning and mix well. Divide the mixture into 16 balls and lightly coat in flour.

Melt the dripping in a large saucepan and fry the meat balls quickly to brown and then lift them out with a slotted spoon and put on one side.

Stir the contents of the packet of soup mix into the dripping in the pan and then gradually add the water and bring to the boil, stirring until thickened.

Return the meat balls to the pan, cover and simmer for 20 minutes. If necessary add a little extra water if the sauce is too thick.

Serves 4

Cheddar Spaghetti Bake

This dish is a complete meal in itself, but, if you like, serve it with a green salad.

Preparation time about 20 minutes
Cooking time about 40 minutes

½ oz (12.5 g) dripping
1 onion, chopped
1 green pepper, seeded and cut in strips
1 lb (450 g) minced beef
6 oz (175 g) spaghetti
¼ level teaspoon dried thyme
salt and pepper
14-oz (397-g) can peeled tomatoes
2 oz (50 g) Cheddar cheese, grated

Heat the oven to 350°F, 180°C, gas mark 4.

Melt the dripping in a saucepan add the onion, green pepper and mince and fry for about 15 minutes.

Meanwhile, cook the spaghetti in plenty of fast boiling salted water for 12 minutes or until tender. Rinse and drain thoroughly.

Add the thyme and plenty of seasoning to the meat.

Grease a 3-pint (1.7-litre) ovenproof dish and put in half the meat mixture, cover with half the contents of the can of tomatoes and then half the spaghetti. Repeat with the remaining meat, tomatoes and spaghetti.

Cover the dish and bake in the oven for 30 minutes. Remove the lid and sprinkle over the cheese. Return to the oven without the lid for a further 10 minutes, so that the cheese melts.

Serves 4

Curried Beef Turnovers

Meat pasties are always popular with men – and children, too – and the addition of curry gives them a special lift.

Preparation time about 20 minutes
Cooking time about 25 to 30 minutes

½ oz (12.5 g) butter
1 to 2 level teaspoons curry powder
half a green pepper, chopped
1 oz (25 g) plain flour
15-oz (425-g) can minced beef and onions
14-oz (397-g) packet shortcrust pastry
milk

Melt the butter in a small saucepan and add the curry powder and green pepper and fry gently for 4 minutes. Stir in the flour and the can of minced beef and onions and bring to the boil, stirring, and cook until thickened. Turn the mixture out onto a plate and leave to cool.

Heat the oven to 400°F, 200°C, gas mark 6.

Roll out the pastry to form two 11-inch (27.5-cm) squares and cut each square into four smaller squares. Divide the filling between the pastry squares. Damp the edges and then fold over to form triangles. Seal the edges firmly.

Put the turnovers on a baking tray and make a small slit in the centre of each for the steam to escape. Brush over with a little milk and bake in the oven for 25 to 30 minutes until pastry is cooked and a pale golden brown.

Makes 8 turnovers

Baked Meat Loaf

In winter, eat this meat loaf hot with potatoes and vegetables; in summer, bake the loaf and leave it to get quite cold, then slice it thinly and serve with a selection of salads.

Preparation time about 5 minutes
Cooking time about 1 hour

2 oz (50 g) fresh breadcrumbs
1 medium-sized onion, chopped
¼ level teaspoon mixed dried herbs
1 level teaspoon salt
freshly ground black pepper
2 teaspoons Worcestershire sauce
1 level tablespoon tomato ketchup
1 egg
1 lb (450 g) minced beef

Heat the oven to 350°F, 180°C, gas mark 4.

Mix all the ingredients together very thoroughly and turn into a 1-pint, (600-ml) loaf tin. Press down firmly and bake in the oven for 1 hour.

If serving hot, turn out onto a serving dish and serve with gravy or a sauce. If serving cold, leave to cool in the tin before turning out.

Serves 4 to 6

Spaghetti with Meat Sauce

This is a quick and easy meat sauce to serve with spaghetti when unexpected visitors pop in. Use a brown onion soup mix, sometimes called French Onion Soup.

Preparation time about 10 minutes
Cooking time about 45 minutes

½ oz (12.5 g) dripping
1 lb (450 g) minced beef
1-pint (600-ml) packet onion soup mix
8-oz (227-g) can peeled tomatoes
1 level tablespoon tomato purée
½ pint (300 ml) water
¼ level teaspoon mixed dried herbs
8 oz (225 g) spaghetti
oil

Melt the dripping in a saucepan, add the beef and fry for 3 to 4 minutes to allow the fat to run out. Stir in the contents of the packet of soup mix together with the tomatoes, purée, water and herbs and bring to the boil, stirring. Partially cover the pan and simmer for 45 minutes or until the beef is tender. Taste and, if necessary, add seasoning to taste.

Meanwhile, cook the spaghetti in fast boiling water, with salt added as directed on the packet. Rinse and drain well. Add a little oil to the spaghetti pan, heat, add the spaghetti and toss thoroughly in the oil.

Arrange the spaghetti on a warm serving dish and spoon over the meat sauce. If liked, serve with a bowl of grated cheese.

Serves 4

Minced Beef Cobbler

Putting a cobbler topping on top of mince means that there is no need to serve potatoes. Serve with braised celery and carrots.

Preparation time about 15 minutes
Cooking time about 50 minutes

    ½ oz (12.5 g) dripping
    1 onion, chopped
    1 lb (450 g) minced beef
    1½ oz (40 g) flour
    1 beef stock cube
    ¾ pint (450 ml) water
    salt and pepper
    8-oz (227-g) packet frozen mixed vegetables

Cobbler topping
    6 oz (175 g) self-raising flour
    ½ level teaspoon salt
    2 oz (50 g) margarine
    6 to 7 tablespoons milk

Melt the dripping in a saucepan, add the onion and mince and fry for 5 minutes. Stir in the flour and cook for 1 minute. Add the stock cube, water and plenty of seasoning and bring to the boil, stirring. Partially cover and simmer for 30 minutes. Stir in the mixed vegetables and turn into an ovenproof dish.

Heat the oven to 400°F, 200°C, gas mark 6.

While the mince is cooking, prepare the cobbler: put the flour and salt into a bowl and rub in the margarine until the mixture resembles breadcrumbs. Stir in the milk to make a soft but not sticky dough, turn onto a floured surface and knead lightly until smooth. Roll out to ¾-inch (2-cm) thickness and cut into 12 rounds with a 2-inch (5-cm) cutter. Brush each round with a little milk and then arrange on top of the mince. Bake for 20 to 25 minutes until golden brown.

Serves 4

Somerset Meat Balls

Cider added to the sauce gives it a lovely flavour, and beer could be used too. Serve these meat balls with creamy mashed potato to absorb the sauce.

Preparation time about 20 minutes
Cooking time about 20 to 30 minutes

1 lb (450 g) minced beef
3 oz (75 g) fresh white breadcrumbs
1 egg
1 teaspoon salt
pepper
1 oz (25 g) flour
1 oz (25 g) dripping
1 large onion, sliced
1 large carrot, sliced
¼ pint (150 ml) dry cider
¼ pint (150 ml) beef stock
2 tablespoons tomato purée
salt and pepper

Put the beef, breadcrumbs, egg and seasoning into a bowl and mix well. Divide the mixture into 20 balls and coat each in flour.

Melt the dripping in a large saucepan and fry the meat balls quickly to brown and then lift them out with a slotted spoon. Add the onion and carrot to the pan and fry for 3 to 4 minutes, then stir in any remaining flour and cook for 1 minute. Blend in the cider and stock and bring to the boil, stirring. Add the tomato purée and seasoning and mix well.

Return the meat balls to the saucepan, cover with a tight fitting lid and simmer gently for 20 to 30 minutes. Taste and check seasoning and turn into a warm serving dish.

Serves 4

Bitkis

Bitkis are small beef cakes that are cooked in tomato sauce and served with a little soured cream or yogurt.

Preparation time about 15 minutes
Cooking time about 30 minutes

1 lb (450 g) minced beef
1 onion, very finely chopped
1 tablespoon chopped parsley
1 level teaspoon salt
freshly ground black pepper
4 oz (100 g) white bread with the crusts removed
¼ pint (150 ml) water
flour
1 tablespoon oil
10½-oz (298-g) can condensed cream of tomato soup
2 tablespoons water
2 to 3 tablespoons soured cream or natural yogurt

Heat the oven to 350°F, 180°C, gas mark 4.

Put the beef, onion, parsley and seasoning in a bowl. Cut the bread into small pieces and put in another bowl with the ¼ pint (150 ml) water, and leave to soak for 5 minutes or until all the water has been absorbed. Add the bread to the meat and mix until blended.

Shape the mixture firmly into 12 cakes and coat with flour. Heat the oil in a large pan and fry the cakes quickly to brown on both sides. Lift them out and put in a single layer in a shallow ovenproof dish.

Put the soup in the pan with the water and heat through, then pour over the beef cakes. Cover with a lid or piece of foil and cook in the oven for 30 minutes until the cakes are no longer pink in the middle, then stir in the soured cream or yogurt and serve.

Serves 4

Quick Chilli Con Carne

A chilli is ideal for instant informal entertaining, and just the sort of meal you can produce from ingredients in the store cupboard when friends arrive.

Making time about 25 minutes

2 tablespoons oil
1 large onion, sliced
1 large green pepper, sliced
15-oz (425-g) can minced beef
14-oz (397-g) can peeled tomatoes
15¼-oz (432-g) can dark red kidney beans, drained
1 level teaspoon chilli powder
salt
freshly ground black pepper

Heat the oil in a saucepan, add the onion and green pepper and fry for 5 minutes.

Add all the remaining ingredients and bring to the boil, stirring. Cover and simmer gently for 20 minutes. Taste and check seasoning and serve with plain boiled rice.

Serves 4

Potato Burgers

Adding potatoes to burgers makes them go a very long way and also gives a good flavour and texture.

Preparation time about 15 minutes
Cooking time about 10 minutes per batch

1 lb (450 g) potatoes, peeled
1 lb (450 g) good quality minced beef
1 egg, beaten
2 tablespoons tomato ketchup
2 teaspoons Worcestershire sauce
1½ level teaspoons salt
plenty of freshly ground black pepper
1 medium-sized onion, grated
a little lard or dripping for frying

Grate the potatoes on a medium grater and drain off any liquid. If necessary, dry the potato on kitchen paper.

Put all the ingredients except the lard or dripping into a large bowl and mix together very thoroughly. Divide the mixture into 20 pieces and roughly shape into burgers about 3 inches (7.5 cm) in diameter and ¼ inch (6 mm) thick.

Heat the lard or dripping in a frying pan and fry the burgers over a moderate heat for 5 minutes on each side. Lift out and keep warm while cooking the remaining burgers.

Makes about 20 burgers

Potato Goulash

A potato goulash is almost a complete meal in itself. If you like, serve it with a green vegetable, such as green beans or peas.

Preparation time about 10 minutes
Cooking time about 45 minutes

½ oz (12.5 g) dripping
2 onions, chopped
1 lb (450 g) minced beef
1½-pint (900-ml) packet tomato soup mix
¾ pint (450 ml) water
2 teaspoons Worcestershire sauce
1 level tablespoon paprika pepper
1 level teaspoon salt
1 green pepper, seeded and cut into strips
1½ lb (675 g) potatoes

Melt the dripping in a saucepan. Add the onions and minced beef and fry for 3 to 4 minutes to let the fat run out of the meat.

Stir the contents of the soup mix packet into the meat and add the water, Worcestershire sauce, paprika pepper, salt and green pepper. Bring to the boil, stirring. Reduce the heat, cover the pan and simmer for about 45 minutes until the meat is tender.

Meanwhile, cook the potatoes in boiling salted water until tender, then drain and cut into slices. Put slices in the base of a casserole and keep warm.

Taste the goulash and check seasoning, then pour over the potatoes. Serve very hot.

Serves 4

Corned Beef Hash

This is one of the best ways of serving a can of corned beef. Hash is quick to make and a great favourite with the children.

Making time about 25 minutes

1 oz (25 g) dripping
1 large onion, chopped
1½ lb (675 g) potatoes, peeled and diced
½ pint (300 ml) milk
salt
freshly ground black pepper
12-oz (340-g) can corned beef, diced

Melt the dripping in a large frying pan, then add the onion and fry for 3 to 4 minutes. Add the potatoes and fry for 1 minute, then pour in the milk and seasoning. Cover and simmer for about 10 minutes or until the potatoes are tender.

Add the corned beef to the pan and continue cooking gently, turning the contents of the pan occasionally with a fish slice. As the hash cooks the potatoes will absorb the milk and the corned beef and potatoes will blend together and become brown and crispy. This will take about 10 to 15 minutes.

Turn into a hot dish and serve.

Serves 4

BACON

Bacon chops and steaks go well with a good tomato sauce. Use condensed tomato soup for a short cut. Left-over pieces of a bacon joint combine happily with cheese, eggs, pasta or rice for a very quick supper dish.

Bacon Chops with Rice

All you need to serve with this recipe is a crisp green salad or a dish of buttered courgettes.

Preparation time about 20 minutes
Cooking time about 25–30 minutes

  4 oz (100 g) long grain rice
  1 oz (25 g) butter
  1 tablespoon oil
  1 medium-sized onion, chopped
  4 oz (100 g) carrots
  4 oz (100 g) celery, sliced
  1 rounded tablespoon chopped parsley
  1 level teaspoon paprika pepper
  salt
  freshly ground black pepper
  14½-oz (410-g) can pineapple chunks
  4 bacon steaks

Heat the oven to 375°F, 190°C, gas mark 5. Grease a shallow oven-proof dish.

Cook the rice in fast boiling salted water for 12 minutes or until tender. Rinse and drain well.

Meanwhile, heat the butter and oil in a saucepan and fry the onion, carrots and celery for 10 minutes.

Stir the rice, parsley, paprika pepper and salt and pepper into the vegetables and mix lightly. Drain the juice from the pineapple and add the chunks to the rice mixture. Stir the rice mixture through with a fork and place in the ovenproof dish. Lay the bacon steaks on top, cover with a piece of foil and bake in the oven for 25 to 30 minutes. Serve at once.

Serves 4

Macaroni Cheese with Bacon

Macaroni is just one of the pastas to choose from. Try pasta shells or bows for a change.

Preparation time about 20 minutes
Cooking time about 20 minutes

> *6 oz (175 g) short-cut macaroni*
> *2 oz (50 g) butter*
> *2 oz (50 g) flour*
> *1½ pints (675 ml) milk*
> *salt*
> *freshly ground black pepper*
> *6 oz (175 g) Cheddar cheese, grated*
> *8 rashers streaky bacon*

Heat the oven to 425°F, 220°c, gas mark 7. Butter an ovenproof dish.

Cook the macaroni in boiling salted water until just tender, according to the directions on the packet. This will take about 10 to 12 minutes. Drain well.

Melt the butter in a saucepan, stir in the flour and cook for 1 minute. Add the milk and bring to the boil, stirring until the sauce has thickened. Simmer for 1 minute.

Remove the pan from the heat, add the seasoning, 4 oz (100 g) of the cheese and the macaroni. Turn the mixture into the ovenproof dish, sprinkle with the rest of the cheese and put in the oven and cook for about 20 minutes until golden brown and hot through.

Meanwhile, remove the rind from the bacon rashers and form into rolls. Put bacon rolls on a small dish and bake in the oven alongside the macaroni cheese for about 15 minutes until a pale golden brown.

Serves 4

Bacon with Tomato and Parsley Sauce

This is very quick and easy to make. Add plenty of fresh chopped parsley to the sauce and serve with buttered noodles.

Preparation time about 5 minutes
Cooking time 1 hour

  1 lb (450 g) pre-packed bacon joint that needs no soaking
  10½-oz (298-g) can condensed tomato soup
  1 soup can of water
  freshly ground black pepper
  plenty of chopped fresh parsley

Remove the wrappings from the bacon joint.

Put the soup in a small saucepan with the water and stir until blended. Add the bacon joint and season well with plenty of freshly ground black pepper. Cover the saucepan and simmer gently for 1 hour.

Lift out the bacon, carve into slices and arrange on a serving dish.

Add the parsley to the sauce, taste and check seasoning and then spoon over the bacon.

Serves 4

Bacon Steaks with Spicy Tomato Sauce

To make this dish a complete meal, serve it with a green vegetable such as broccoli or French beans.

Preparation time about 15 minutes
Cooking time about 25 minutes

1 large packet, 4½ oz (131 g), instant mashed potato
4 bacon steaks

Sauce
14-oz (397-g) can peeled tomatoes
1 teaspoon Worcestershire sauce
1 small clove of garlic, crushed
1 small onion, finely chopped
2 teaspoons vinegar
½ level teaspoon dry mustard
1 tablespoon honey

Heat the oven to 350°F, 180°C, gas mark 4.

Place all the sauce ingredients together in a saucepan, bring to the boil and then reduce the heat and simmer for 15 minutes.

Meanwhile, make up the mashed potato as directed on the packet. Make a border of mashed potato around the edge of an ovenproof dish and lay the bacon steaks, slightly overlapping, down the centre of the dish. Taste and check seasoning of the sauce, spoon over the bacon and cook in the oven for 20 to 25 minutes.

Serves 4

Ham and Leeks in Cheese Sauce

Make this supper dish when leeks are at their best and still small. Serve with French bread or granary rolls.

Preparation time about 20 minutes
Cooking time about 5 to 8 minutes

8 small leeks
1½ oz (40 g) butter
1½ oz (40 g) flour
¾ pint (450 ml) milk
4 oz (100 g) Cheddar cheese, grated
½ teaspoon made mustard
salt and pepper
8 slices cooked ham
½ oz (12.5 g) grated Parmesan cheese

Remove the coarse outer leaves from the leeks and cut off the tops and roots. Wash very thoroughly, splitting the leeks to within 1 inch (2.5 cm) of base to remove all grit. Cook in boiling salted water for about 15 minutes until tender.

Meanwhile, melt the butter in a saucepan, then stir in the flour and cook for 1 minute. Blend in the milk and bring to the boil, stirring. Simmer for 2 minutes or until the sauce has thickened. Add 3 oz (75 g) Cheddar cheese to the sauce together with mustard and seasoning.

Thoroughly drain the leeks and wrap a slice of ham around each leek. Place leeks in a single layer in a shallow ovenproof dish, then spoon over the sauce and sprinkle with the remaining Cheddar cheese and the Parmesan cheese.

Brown under a hot grill and serve at once.

Serves 4

Glazed Orange Bacon Steaks

This is an unusual and simple way of serving bacon steaks, and it can be easily adapted to serve any number of people.

Preparation time about 10 minutes
Cooking time about 25 minutes

4 bacon steaks
Dijon mustard
about 4 oz (100 g) light soft brown sugar
2 small oranges

Heat the oven to 350°F, 180°C, gas mark 4.

Spread each bacon steak with mustard and roll in the soft brown sugar. Lay steaks in a single layer in an ovenproof dish. Cut 1 orange into 8 slices and lay 2 slices on top of each bacon steak. Squeeze the juice from the remaining orange and pour over the bacon.

Bake in the oven for about 25 minutes, when the sauce will be golden brown and syrupy. It is a good idea to baste occasionally during cooking time.

Serves 4

Pasta Savoury

A Pasta Savoury is an ideal way to use up the last pieces of a ham or bacon joint, adding other ingredients which are always in the store cupboard.

Preparation time about 15 minutes
Cooking time about 5 minutes

6 oz (175 g) pasta bows or shells
1 oz (25 g) butter
1 large onion, chopped
10½-oz (298-g) can condensed mushroom or tomato soup
4 oz (100 g) ham pieces
2 oz (50 g) Cheddar cheese, grated

Cook the pasta bows or shells in plenty of fast boiling well-salted water, as directed on the packet. Rinse and drain very thoroughly.

Meanwhile, melt the butter in a saucepan, add the onion and cook gently for about 10 minutes or until the onion is soft but not brown.

Add the pasta to the saucepan together with the soup and ham and stir thoroughly until well mixed. Season to taste.

Turn the mixture into an ovenproof dish and sprinkle with the cheese. Place under a moderate grill for about 5 minutes until the cheese is golden brown and bubbling.

Serves 4

Ham Rosti

Ham Rosti is a filling supper dish which is really a meal in itself. If liked, it can be served with garden peas.

Preparation time about 20 minutes
Cooking time about 40 minutes

2 lb (900 g) large potatoes
1 large onion
½ level teaspoon salt
freshly ground black pepper
8 oz (225 g) cooked ham or bacon, chopped
2 oz (50 g) dripping

Scrub the potatoes and boil in water for 10 minutes or until the point of a knife can be inserted about 1 inch (2.5 cm) into the potato before meeting resistance. Drain, cool and peel. Grate into a large bowl and then grate in the onion. Add the seasoning and ham and mix thoroughly.

Melt half the dripping in a large non-stick frying pan and add the potato mixture. Flatten the potato with a fish slice and cook very slowly over a low heat for 20 minutes, when the base will be golden brown. Turn out onto a large dish. Melt the remaining dripping in the pan and slide back the rosti to brown on the second side, as before.

Serves 4

Ham Salad Rolls

It is nice to use honey roast ham for this recipe.

Making time about 20 minutes

8-oz (227-g) packet frozen vegetable rice
4 tablespoons thick mayonnaise
1 level tablespoon chopped chives
salt and pepper
4 large slices cooked ham
lettuce
tomato wedges
sprigs of watercress or mustard and cress

Cook the vegetable rice as directed on the packet and then turn into a bowl and cool quickly. Stir in the mayonnaise and chives, mix well and add seasoning to taste.

Lay the ham flat and divide the vegetable mixture between the 4 slices, then roll up. Arrange a bed of lettuce on a serving dish and place the ham rolls on top. Garnish the dish with tomato wedges and sprigs of watercress or a little mustard and cress.

Serves 4

Gammon and Pineapple

Always a great favourite, I find that by adding a little mustard to the glaze it gives it a bit of a lift.

Preparation time about 5 minutes
Cooking time about 12 minutes

4 thick rashers of gammon
3 level tablespoons light soft brown sugar
1 level tablespoon dry mustard
8-oz (227-g) can pineapple rings

Remove the rind from the bacon and cut the fat around the edge, snipping inwards to prevent the edges curling up during cooking.

Put the sugar and mustard in a small bowl. Open the can of pineapple and take sufficient juice to add to the sugar mixture to make a thin glaze.

Heat the grill to moderate and remove the rack from the grill pan. Lay the rashers in the pan and pour over the glaze. Grill for about 5 minutes on each side, turning once. Arrange a pineapple ring on each rasher and return to the grill and heat through.

Place on a warm serving dish and spoon over glaze. Serve with grilled halved tomatoes, if liked.

Serves 4

Stuffed Bacon Rolls

These bacon rolls make a nice change and are good if served with tomato sauce.

Preparation time about 15 minutes
Cooking time about 15 to 20 minutes

1 onion
4 oz (100 g) chicken livers
2 oz (50 g) butter
4 oz (100 g) mushrooms stalks
4 oz (100 g) fresh white breadcrumbs
a little salt
freshly ground black pepper
12 rashers back bacon

Heat the oven to 400°F, 200°C, gas mark 6. Lightly grease a baking sheet or ovenproof dish.

Mince the onion and chicken livers. Heat the butter in a saucepan and fry the onion and chicken livers for 5 minutes, stirring. Mince the mushroom stalks and add them to the pan and cook for 2 minutes. Add the breadcrumbs, a very little salt and black pepper and mix thoroughly. It is not a good idea to add too much salt to the stuffing as bacon can be very salty.

Remove the rind from the bacon and spread flat. Divide the stuffing between the bacon rashers and roll up. Place the rolls on the baking sheet or in the dish and cook in the oven for 15 to 20 minutes. When cooked the bacon will be tender and lightly browned. Lift out and serve in a warm dish.

Serves 4

SAUSAGES AND BURGERS

Sausages are firm favourites with children and menfolk alike, and sausage meat makes excellent flans and pasties to eat hot or cold. The addition of a hot well-flavoured sauce makes either home-made or frozen beefburgers an important dish. Most people like plenty of mustard with them, too.

Banger Bonanza

Chipolata sausages are perfect for this dish as they cook quickly.

Making time about 25 minutes

1 oz (25 g) pork dripping or lard
1 lb (450 g) pork chipolata sausages
1 large onion, chopped
4 rashers streaky bacon, chopped
1 oz (25 g) flour
½ pint (300 ml) beef stock
1 level tablespoon tomato purée
salt and pepper
chopped parsley

Heat the dripping in a large frying pan and fry the sausages, onion and bacon for 5 minutes. Stir in the flour and then gradually add the stock and tomato purée and bring to the boil. Season well, cover the pan and simmer for 15 minutes.

Taste and check seasoning and turn into a warm serving dish. Sprinkle with chopped parsley and serve.

Serves 4

Liver Sausage Puffs

A hot favourite with the children in our family, serve these puffs hot with baked beans or cold with a mixed salad and new potatoes.

Preparation time about 15 minutes
Cooking time about 20 minutes

8-oz (227-g) packet puff pastry
4 oz (100 g) liver sausage
2 level tablespoons tomato ketchup
1 rounded tablespoon finely chopped chives

Heat the oven to 425°F, 220°C, gas mark 7.

Roll out the pastry to make an 11-inch (28-cm) square and then trim the edges and cut into nine 3½-inch (9-cm) squares.

Mash the liver sausage with the tomato ketchup and chives in a small bowl. Place a spoonful of the filling on each piece of pastry. Damp the edges and fold the pastry in half to form a triangle. Press the edges firmly together.

Place the puffs on a baking tray and brush with a little milk. Make a small slit in the top of each and bake in the oven for 20 minutes until well risen and golden brown.

Makes 9 puffs

Beefburger Pan Fry

This is a substantial high tea or supper dish that is made all in one pan.

Making time about 20 minutes

1 oz (25 g) dripping
2 beefburgers
1 large onion, cut in rings
8 oz (225 g) cooked potatoes, diced
2 rashers streaky bacon, cut in strips
a little chopped parsley

Melt the dripping in a frying pan and fry the beefburgers and onions together for 5 minutes, turning the beefburgers once. Lift out the beefburgers and put on a warm serving dish.

Add the potatoes and bacon to the pan and quickly fry until the potatoes are brown, turning frequently.

Spoon the potato and onion mixture around the beefburgers and sprinkle with a little chopped parsley.

Serves 2

Creole Sausages

Try serving sausages this way for a change. There is plenty of sauce so ideally serve them with creamy mashed potato.

Making time about 30 minutes

½ oz (12.5 g) dripping
1 lb (450 g) pork sausages
1 medium-sized onion, chopped
2 sticks celery, sliced
14-oz (397-g) can peeled tomatoes
2 teaspoons Worcestershire sauce
¼ pint (150 ml) stock
salt and pepper

Melt the dripping in a frying pan and fry the sausages for 10 minutes to brown all over. Lift out with a slotted spoon and keep warm.

Add the onion and celery to the pan and fry for 5 minutes to brown, then strain off any excess fat and stir in the remaining ingredients and bring to the boil.

Return the sausages to the pan and simmer for 10 minutes. Turn into a serving dish.

Serves 4

Beefburgers in Mushroom Cider Sauce

If you are not short of time, make your own beefburgers for this dish.

Preparation time about 10 minutes
Cooking time about 8 to 10 minutes

1 oz (25 g) butter
8 beefburgers
1 onion, chopped
1 oz (25 g) flour
¼ pint (150 ml) cider
½ pint (300 ml) water
1 beef stock cube
salt and pepper
chopped parsley
6 oz (175 g) mushrooms, sliced

Melt the butter in a large frying pan, then add the beefburgers and fry quickly for 1 minute on each side. Lift out with a slotted spoon.

Add the onion to the pan and fry for 3 to 4 minutes. Stir in the flour and cook for 1 minute. Blend in the cider and water and stock cube and bring to the boil, stirring. Season well and return the beefburgers to the pan with the parsley and mushrooms. Cover and simmer for 8 to 10 minutes.

Turn onto a serving dish and serve with creamy mashed potato and sliced carrots.

Serves 4

Beefburgers with Mustard Cream Sauce

So simple, the mustard sauce really gives the beefburgers a tremendous lift and makes them special enough for an impromptu supper party.

Making time about 12 minutes

 4 frozen beefburgers
 1 oz (25 g) butter
 ¼ pint (150 ml) double cream
 1 level tablespoon Dijon mustard
 a few drops of Worcestershire sauce
 salt and pepper

Fry the beefburgers according to the directions on the packet, but fry them in the butter. Lift the beefburgers from the pan and place on a warm serving dish.

Meanwhile, blend the cream with the mustard and Worcestershire sauce and seasoning.

Add the cream to the pan and heat through, stirring gently, until hot but not boiling. Taste and check seasoning, then pour over the beefburgers. Serve at once with broccoli and grilled tomatoes.

Serves 4

Savoury Flan

If you like, use frozen shortcrust pastry. Serve with a mixed salad and new potatoes.

Preparation time about 25 to 30 minutes
Cooking time about 40 minutes

Pastry
   6 oz (175 g) plain flour
   1½ oz (40 g) margarine
   1½ oz (40 g) lard
   about 6 teaspoons cold water to mix

Filling
   4 oz (100 g) streaky bacon
   4 oz (100 g) mushrooms, sliced
   1 medium-sized onion, chopped
   1 lb (450 g) pork sausage meat
   1 level tablespoon chopped parsley
   salt
   ground black pepper
   salt and pepper
   4 eggs, beaten

Put the flour in a bowl. Add the fats, cut in small pieces, and rub in with the fingertips until the mixture resembles fine breadcrumbs. Add sufficient cold water to mix to a firm dough and then roll out and line a 9-inch (22.5-cm) deep flan tin. Chill.

Heat the oven to 425°F, 220°C, gas mark 7.

Remove the rind and any bone from the bacon and cut in strips. Put in a frying pan with the mushrooms and onion and fry for 5 minutes. Stir in the pork sausage meat and mix well together. Add the parsley and a little salt and ground black pepper. Spread the filling over the base of the flan and smooth flat with the back of a spoon. Add a little seasoning to the eggs and pour over the flan. Bake in the oven for 40 minutes.

Serves 6

Macaroni Supper Dish

A popular dish with the young that can be ready to eat in half an hour.

Preparation time about 10 minutes
Cooking time about 25 minutes

  1 lb (450 g) pork sausage meat
  flour
  ½ oz (12.5 g) dripping
  6 oz (175 g) quick cook macaroni
  1-pint (600-ml) packet mushroom soup mix
  ¾ pint (450 ml) water
  1 level tablespoon tomato purée
  8-oz (227-g) packet peas, sweetcorn and peppers, cooked

Shape the sausage meat into 15 small balls and coat in flour. Melt the dripping in a large frying pan and fry the sausage meat balls for about 10 minutes until golden brown all over.

Meanwhile, cook the macaroni as directed on the packet and drain thoroughly.

Rinse out the saucepan, add the soup mix and water and bring to the boil, stirring until thickened. Add the tomato purée and peas, sweetcorn and peppers and mix well. Stir in the macaroni and heat through until the mixture is piping hot. Taste and check seasoning, then pile the macaroni onto a warm serving dish and arrange the sausage meat balls on top. Serve at once.

Serves 4

Sausage Splits

If liked, instead of filling the sausages with cheese, use a spoonful of thick spicy chutney. I find that these sausage splits are very popular served with a large helping of baked beans in tomato sauce.

Preparation time about 5 to 10 minutes
Cooking time about 15 to 20 minutes

> 1 lb (450 g) large pork or beef sausages
> 4 oz (100 g) Cheddar cheese, in one piece
> 8 rashers streaky bacon

Heat the grill to moderate.

Split each sausage lengthwise, cut the cheese into eight fingers and place one finger in each sausage.

Remove the rind and any bone from each rasher of bacon and wrap around each sausage spiral fashion. Secure with a wooden cocktail stick.

Cook under the grill for 15 to 20 minutes, turning frequently, until the bacon is golden brown and the cheese has melted.

Remove the cocktail sticks and arrange the sausages on a warm serving dish.

Serves 4

Ploughman's Pasty

This is simple to make, and left-overs are very good served cold with a salad.

Preparation time about 10 minutes
Cooking time about 30 minutes

　1 lb (450 g) pork sausage meat
　10½-oz (298-g) can condensed vegetable soup
　8-oz (227-g) packet puff pastry
　milk to glaze

Heat the oven to 425°F, 220°C, gas mark 7.

Put the sausage meat and soup in a bowl and mix well together.

Cut the pastry in half and roll out each piece to form a 9-inch (22.5-cm) square. Place one piece of pastry on an ovenproof dish or baking tray. Spread the sausage meat filling over the pastry to within 1 inch (2.5 cm) of the edge. Brush the edge with a little milk and then cover with the remaining piece of pastry. Seal the edges very firmly.

Make two slits in the centre of the pastry to allow the steam to escape, and brush all over with milk. Bake the pasty in the oven for 30 minutes until golden brown. Serve warm with a good gravy.

Serves 8

Sausage Saxony

Try serving sausages in this delicious rich sauce for a change. Sausage Saxony should be accompanied with noodles or boiled rice.

Preparation time about 10 minutes
Cooking time about 10 minutes

> *1 tablespoon oil*
> *1 lb (450 g) large pork sausages*
> *2 large onions, chopped*
> *2 rashers streaky bacon, chopped*
> *10½-oz (298-g) can condensed oxtail soup*
> *half a soup can of water*
> *½ teaspoon mixed dried herbs*
> *salt and pepper*

Heat the oil in a frying pan, and fry the sausages gently to brown all over. Lift sausages out of the pan and pour off all but a tablespoon of the fat. Add the onion and bacon to the pan and fry quickly for 5 minutes. Add the soup, water, herbs and seasoning and bring to the boil, stirring.

Return the sausages to the pan and simmer for a further 10 minutes.

Taste and check seasoning, then turn into a warm serving dish.

Serves 4

Kate's Kebabs

These kebabs are easy to make and can be prepared quite simply by a child.

Preparation time about 10 minutes
Cooking time about 10 to 12 minutes

8 rashers streaky bacon
8 chipolata sausages
1 green pepper
2 large tomatoes
8 button mushrooms
8-oz (227-g) can pineapple cubes, drained

Baste
2 tablespoons oil
1 tablespoon Worcestershire sauce
2 teaspoons tomato ketchup

Heat the grill and lightly oil four long skewers.

Remove the rind and bone from the bacon and roll up firmly. Twist each sausage in half and then cut so that you have 16 small sausages. Cut the pepper in half, remove the seeds and white pith and cut each half into four neat squares. Quarter the tomatoes and remove the seeds.

On each skewer put 2 bacon rolls, 4 small sausages, 2 pieces of green pepper, 2 quarters of tomato, two mushrooms and 3 pineapple cubes. The ingredients may be arranged in any order you like.

Mix all the baste ingredients together and brush over the kebabs. Grill for 10 to 12 minutes, turning and brushing with a little extra baste during cooking.

Serve the kebabs on a bed of rice with a green salad.

Serves 4

Luncheon Meat with Sweetcorn Fritters

Instead of luncheon meat you could use eight rashers of back bacon or four bacon steaks.

Preparation time about 5 minutes
Cooking time about 10 minutes

> 12-oz (340-g) can luncheon meat
> 2 tablespoons oil

Fritters
> 2 oz (50 g) self-raising flour
> 1 egg, beaten
> 4 tablespoons milk
> salt and pepper
> 7-oz (198-g) can mexicorn, well drained

Cut the luncheon meat into 8 neat slices. Heat the oil in a frying pan and quickly fry the luncheon meat until golden brown on both sides. Lift out and arrange on a serving dish and keep warm.

Put the flour in a bowl, make a well in the centre, add the egg, milk and seasoning and mix to a smooth batter. Stir in the mexicorn and then fry in 8 spoonfuls in the frying pan for about 2 to 3 minutes on each side, until golden brown and puffed up.

Serves 4

Beefburger Pasties

For a change try spreading the beefburgers with horseradish sauce instead of chutney and using a thin apple ring instead of the sliced tomato.

Preparation time about 20 minutes
Cooking time about 25 minutes

8-oz (227-g) packet puff pastry, thawed
4 beefburgers
2 level tablespoons chutney or relish
4 slices tomato
beaten egg or milk to glaze

Heat the oven to 425°F, 220°C, gas mark 7.

Roll out the pastry thinly and cut out eight 5-inch (12.5-cm) circles, using a small saucer as a guide.

Lay the beefburgers on four of the pastry circles and spread with chutney or relish. Lay a tomato slice on top.

Brush the edges of the pastry with beaten egg or milk and then cover with the remaining pastry. Seal the edges firmly, make a slit in the top of each pasty and glaze with the remaining egg or milk.

Place pasties on a baking tray and bake in the oven for about 20 to 25 minutes until the pastry is well risen and golden brown.

Serves 4

OFFAL

Liver and kidneys make ideal quick meals because they need only a
short cooking time – liver in particular should never be over-cooked.
Another recommendation that should not be dismissed is that offal is
comparatively cheap.

Mild Devilled Kidneys with Pasta

Serve with buttered broccoli or beans to make a complete meal.

Preparation time about 12 minutes
Cooking time about 15 minutes

8 to 12 lambs' kidneys, depending on the size
about ½ oz (12.5 g) seasoned flour
1 medium-sized onion, sliced
6 rashers streaky bacon, chopped
2 tablespoons oil
2 oz (50 g) butter
14-oz (397-g) can peeled tomatoes
1 tablespoon tomato purée
½ pint (300 ml) stock
¼ pint (150 ml) cider
1 tablespoon Worcestershire sauce
4 oz (100 g) pasta bows or shells
salt
freshly ground black pepper

Skin the kidneys, cut them in half horizontally and snip out the cores with a pair of scissors. Coat them in the seasoned flour.

In a saucepan, fry the onion and bacon in the oil and butter for 2 to 3 minutes. Add the prepared kidneys and fry for 1 minute to seal them.

Add the canned tomatoes, purée, stock, cider and Worcestershire sauce to the pan and bring to the boil. Stir in the pasta with the seasoning and then cover the saucepan and simmer gently for about 15 minutes until the pasta is cooked and just tender.

Stir well and turn the kidneys and the sauce into a warm serving dish and allow to stand in a warm place for about 5 minutes to thicken up the sauce slightly.

Serves 4

Chicken Liver Vol-au-vents

This is a delicious way to serve chicken livers. Cook whole tomatoes, crossed on top, in the oven while you bake the vol-au-vents.

Preparation time about 20 minutes
Cooking time about 25 minutes

7½-oz (212-g) packet uncooked medium-sized vol-au-vents
1 oz (25 g) butter
1 onion, chopped
8 oz (225 g) chicken livers, chopped
4 oz (100 g) mushrooms, chopped
1 oz (25 g) flour
¼ pint (150 ml) chicken stock
salt and pepper

Heat the oven to 425°F, 220°C, gas mark 7. Cook the vol-au-vents as directed on the packet, then remove them from the oven and scoop out the centres.

Meanwhile, make the filling. Melt the butter in a saucepan and add the onion and chicken livers and fry for 3 to 4 minutes, then stir in the mushrooms and cook for another 3 minutes. Add the flour and cook for 1 minute, then blend in the stock and bring to the boil, stirring until thickened. Season well.

Divide the mixture between the vol-au-vent cases and, if liked, pop them back into the oven for about 5 minutes to heat through.

Serve with garden peas and baked tomatoes.

Serves 4 to 6

Braised Liver with Mushrooms

This is very good if served with buttered noodles to absorb the sauce.

Preparation time about 5 minutes
Cooking time about 5 minutes

1 lb (450 g) lambs' liver
1 tablespoon seasoned flour
2 oz (50 g) butter
4 oz (100 g) mushrooms, thinly sliced
14-oz (397-g) can peeled tomatoes
¼ pint (150 ml) cider
salt and pepper

Cut the liver into neat slices and remove any arteries. Coat in the seasoned flour.

Melt the butter in a frying pan and fry the liver for 1 minute on each side to seal the juices, then lift out with a slotted spoon. Add the mushrooms, tomatoes and cider to the pan and bring to the boil, stirring, and season well.

Return the liver to the pan and simmer for about 5 minutes or until the liver is just tender and still slightly pink in the centre. Do not over-cook as long cooking makes it tough.

Taste the sauce and check the seasoning. Turn at once into a warm dish and serve immediately.

Serves 4

Liver and Bacon

A classic English dish. Use calves' liver if available, if not buy lambs' liver cut in thin slices.

Preparation time about 5 minutes
Cooking time about 15 minutes

1 lb (450 g) calves' or lambs' liver, sliced
back bacon rashers, allow 1 for each slice of liver
a little butter
a little seasoned flour

Trim any arteries from the liver. Remove the rind from the bacon rashers.

Heat a little butter in a large frying pan and fry the bacon for 4 to 5 minutes over a moderate heat until it is cooked and fat has run out. Lift out with a slotted spoon and keep warm.

Coat the liver in seasoned flour and then fry it in the fat in the pan for about 3 minutes on each side. When cooked, the liver should still be slightly pink. Over-cooked liver will tend to be dry and tough.

Lift out the liver and place on a warm serving dish with the rashers of bacon. Serve at once as liver should never be kept warm and waiting.

Serves 4 to 6

Kidney and Bacon Pie

This is a filling and warming way to serve kidneys on a winter's day.

Preparation time about 20 minutes
Cooking time about 20 to 25 minutes

  6 lambs' kidneys
  4 oz (100 g) back bacon
  1 tablespoon oil
  ½ oz (12.5 g) butter
  10½-oz (298-g) can condensed mushroom soup
  2½ fl oz (75 ml) water
  8 oz (225 g) mushrooms, quartered
  salt and pepper
  8-oz (227-g) packet puff pastry
  milk or beaten egg to glaze

Heat the oven to 425°F, 220°C, gas mark 7.

Skin the kidneys and cut them in half horizontally. Snip out the cores with a pair of scissors and cut each piece in half. Remove the rind from the bacon and cut it into thin strips.

Heat the oil and butter in a frying pan and fry the kidneys and bacon for 5 minutes or until almost cooked. Add the soup, water, mushrooms and seasoning and bring to the boil, stirring. Simmer for 2 minutes and turn into a 2½-pint (1.4-litre) pie dish.

Roll out the pastry on a floured surface until it is slightly larger than the dish. Trim it to size and place the trimmings on the rim of the dish, then moisten them with water and put the lid on the pie. Seal firmly and flute the edges and decorate with pastry leaves, if liked. Glaze with milk or beaten egg and make two small slits in the centre. Bake for 20 to 25 minutes or until the pastry is golden brown and well risen.

Serves 4

Kidney Kebabs with Spicy Sauce

Serve the kebabs with plain boiled rice and a crisp green salad tossed in French dressing.

Preparation time about 10 minutes
Cooking time about 15 minutes

8 lambs' kidneys
12 rashers streaky bacon

Spicy sauce
10½-oz (298-g) can condensed cream of tomato soup
1 rounded tablespoon redcurrant jelly
2 teaspoons Worcestershire sauce
2 teaspoons lemon juice
salt and pepper

Skin the kidneys, cut them in half horizontally and snip out the cores with a pair of scissors or a sharp knife. Remove the rind and any gristle from the bacon rashers and roll them up.

Lightly oil four long skewers and on each alternately place 4 kidney halves and 3 bacon rolls.

Heat the grill to moderate to hot.

Place the kebabs on the grill rack and grill for about 15 minutes, turning regularly.

Meanwhile, heat half the soup in a small saucepan with the remaining ingredients, stirring well so that the jelly dissolves. Stir in the rest of the soup and serve the sauce warm with the kebabs.

Serves 4

POULTRY

Chicken joints make marvellously quick suppers. They need very little preparation and don't take long to cook. In addition there is an endless variety of ways in which to serve them. Herbs, spices, bacon and strongly-flavoured vegetables all go happily with the rather bland chicken meat. Serve chicken portions with rice and a tossed green salad, and use condensed or packet soups to make a quick sauce. If you have any left-over cooked chicken then you can easily make a good quick curry.

Turkey portions are widely obtainable nowadays and these may be used in the same way as chicken.

Chicken with Pineapple and Cider Sauce

I like to serve this chicken dish with plain boiled rice to absorb the rather thin pale golden sauce.

Preparation time about 5 minutes
Cooking time about 40 minutes

> 4 chicken joints
> 2 tablespoons oil
> 14½-oz (410-g) can pineapple chunks
> 4 oz (100 g) button mushrooms, quartered
> ¼ pint (150 ml) dry cider
> salt
> freshly ground black pepper

Skin the chicken joints. Heat the oil in a frying pan and add the chicken. Cover with a lid or piece of foil and fry the joints gently, turning occasionally, for about 30 minutes until they are golden brown and tender. Lift out and arrange on a warm serving dish and keep warm.

Drain the pineapple and reserve the juice. Add the pineapple chunks to the frying pan with the mushrooms and fry for about 5 minutes, stirring continually, then lift out with a slotted spoon and arrange around the chicken.

Strain off any excess fat from the pan and add the pineapple juice and cider to the remaining juices. Boil rapidly for 2 to 3 minutes. Season the sauce, pour over the chicken and serve.

Serves 4

Chicken Napoli

I like to make this sauce without any thickening and serve it with spaghetti or long grain rice.

Preparation time about 15 minutes
Cooking time about 30 minutes

 1 oz (25 g) butter
 1 tablespoon oil
 4 chicken joints
 1 onion, sliced
 1 green pepper
 14-oz (397-g) can peeled tomatoes
 4 oz (100 g) mushrooms, quartered
 ¼ pint (150 ml) chicken stock
 salt and pepper
 a little sugar

Heat the butter and oil in a large frying pan. Add the chicken joints and onion and fry for 5 minutes, turning the joints until they are a pale golden brown on all sides.

Drain off any excess fat and then add all the remaining ingredients to the frying pan and bring to the boil. Cover the pan with a lid or piece of foil and simmer gently for about 30 minutes or until the chicken is tender.

Taste and check seasoning. Put the chicken joints on a serving dish and spoon the sauce over the top.

Serves 4

Baked Chicken with Courgettes

Make this dish in the summer when courgettes are plentiful and serve it with tiny new potatoes.

Preparation time about 5 minutes
Cooking time about 45 minutes

4 chicken joints
salt
freshly ground black pepper
3 oz (75 g) butter
1 rounded tablespoon chopped parsley
grated rind and juice of 1 small lemon
1 lb (450 g) courgettes

Heat the oven to 400°F, 200°C, gas mark 6.

Lay the chicken joints in a single layer in a large ovenproof dish or roasting tin. Season well, dot with butter, sprinkle with parsley and lemon rind and pour over the lemon juice. Bake uncovered in the oven for 30 minutes.

Meanwhile, slice the courgettes and put them in a saucepan. Cover them with boiling water, bring to the boil and simmer for 2 minutes. Drain well.

Remove the chicken from the oven and add the courgettes. Turn them in the juices in the dish until well coated and then return the dish to the oven and bake for a further 15 minutes or until both the chicken and the courgettes are tender.

Lift out the chicken joints and place them on a warm serving dish. Spoon the courgettes and juices around.

Serves 4

Chicken and Bacon Fricassee

For a special occasion use a little less milk and add sherry instead.

Preparation time about 10 minutes
Cooking time about 40 minutes

4 chicken joints
freshly ground black pepper
10½-oz (298-g) can condensed mushroom soup
¼ pint (150 ml) milk
4 rashers streaky bacon
fried bread croûtons

Heat the oven to 350°F, 180°C, gas mark 4.

Remove the skin from the chicken and trim off any pieces of fat. Lay the joints in a single layer in a shallow ovenproof dish and season with black pepper.

Put the soup in a small bowl, stir in the milk and then pour over the chicken. Bake uncovered in the oven for 30 minutes.

Remove the rind from the bacon. Place the rashers in an ovenproof dish and put it in the oven alongside the chicken and cook for 10 minutes. Lift the rashers off the dish and arrange one on top of each chicken joint.

Arrange the fried bread croûtons around the edge of the dish and serve with a crisp green salad.

Serves 4

Grilled Garlic and Herb Chicken

This is a very tasty way to serve chicken, and is best made in the summer when there is a good variety of fresh herbs in the garden.

Preparation time about 5 minutes
Cooking time about 30 minutes

   4 oz (100 g) butter
   1 large clove garlic, crushed
   salt
   freshly ground black pepper
   1 level tablespoon fresh chopped parsley
   1 level tablespoon fresh chopped mixed herbs
   4 chicken portions

Remove the rack from the grill pan and heat the grill to moderate.

Put the butter, garlic, seasoning and herbs in a bowl and beat together until well blended.

Make several slashes in the chicken with a sharp pointed knife and spread over half the garlic butter. Cook under the grill for about 15 minutes, basting occasionally.

Turn the chicken over and spread with the remaining butter. Grill for a further 15 minutes or until the chicken is tender. If the juices run clear when the chicken is pricked with a pointed knife then it should be cooked and tender.

Arrange the chicken portions on a warm serving dish and spoon over the juices from the pan.

Serves 4

Creamed Chicken Curry Vol-au-vents

This is a delicious way to serve the last scraps of chicken from the weekend roast.

Making time about 10 minutes

1 oz (25 g) butter
2 level teaspoons mild curry powder, or to taste
½ oz (12.5 g) flour
¼ pint (150 ml) chicken stock
8 oz (225 g) cooked chicken, chopped very finely
¼ pint (150 ml) double cream
salt and pepper
1 level teaspoon made mustard
8 × 2½-inch (6.5-cm) cooked vol-au-vent cases

Melt the butter in a small saucepan, add the curry powder and flour and cook for 1 minute. Stir in the stock and bring to the boil, stirring constantly, then add the chicken and simmer for 5 minutes. Remove the pan from the heat, add the cream, seasoning and mustard. Return to the heat and re-heat but do not boil.

When very hot, spoon the sauce into the warmed vol-au-vent cases and serve at once.

Serves 4

Tipsy Chicken Hot Pot

A very easy and tasty way to serve chicken, this dish is made for informal entertaining. Serve it with a fresh green vegetable such as broccoli or French beans.

Preparation time about 10 minutes
Cooking time about 1 hour

 1 tablespoon oil
 1 oz (25 g) butter
 4 chicken joints
 1 onion, sliced
 10½-oz (298-g) can condensed chicken soup
 ¼ pint (150 ml) cider
 salt and pepper
 1½ lb (675 g) peeled potatoes, thinly sliced and rinsed

Heat the oven to 375°F, 190°C, gas mark 5.

Heat the oil and half of the butter in a large frying pan, then add the chicken joints with the sliced onion and fry for about 5 minutes, turning once to lightly brown the chicken. Lift out and place in a casserole.

Add the soup and cider to the onion in the frying pan and stir well until thoroughly blended. Season and then pour the sauce over the chicken. Arrange the potatoes on top. Cover the casserole and cook in the oven for 30 minutes.

Remove the lid and dot the potatoes with the remaining butter. Return the casserole to the oven without the lid and cook for a further 30 minutes. The potatoes should be a pale golden brown.

Serves 4

Chicken Risotto

This is always a popular dish and will make a little chicken go a long way. Serve it with a bowl of tossed green salad.

Preparation time about 10 minutes
Cooking time about 20 minutes

> 1 oz (25 g) butter
> 1 tablespoon oil
> 4 oz (100 g) streaky bacon, chopped
> 8 oz (225 g) chicken breast, cut in strips
> 1 large onion, chopped
> 8 oz (225 g) long grain rice
> 1 green pepper, seeded and sliced
> 1¼ pints (675 ml) chicken stock
> salt and pepper
> 4 oz (100 g) mushrooms, sliced
> 8 oz (225 g) small tomatoes, peeled and quartered

Heat the butter and oil in a large saucepan and add the bacon, chicken and onion and fry gently for 5 minutes. Stir in the rice and fry for 1 minute so that it absorbs the fat. Add the green pepper, stock and seasoning and bring to the boil, stirring. Cover the pan, reduce the heat and simmer for 15 minutes.

Add the mushrooms to the pan and continue cooking for a further 5 minutes or until the rice is tender and all the stock absorbed.

Taste and check seasoning. Just before serving, stir in the tomatoes very gently so that they get hot through but do not lose their shape.

Turn the risotto into a hot dish and serve at once.

Serves 4

Special Chicken with Lemon and Thyme

So easy, the stuffing thickens the sauce and imparts a herby flavour. If you have no wine to hand you could always use cider.

Preparation time about 8 minutes
Cooking time about 1 hour

  2 tablespoons salad oil
  4 leg portions roasting chicken
  2 rounded tablespoons lemon and thyme packet stuffing mix
  1 large clove garlic, crushed
  14-oz (397-g) can peeled tomatoes
  1 chicken stock cube
  ¼ pint (150 ml) red wine
  1 good tablespoon jam, without seeds
  salt
  freshly ground black pepper

Heat the oven to 350°F, 180°C, gas mark 4.

Heat the oil in a frying pan and fry the chicken so that it is brown on all sides. If liked, remove the chicken skin before frying. Lift out the chicken and put it in a casserole.

Measure all the other ingredients into the frying pan and stir well to incorporate any sediment and to melt the jam. Pour over the chicken, cover the casserole and cook in the oven for about 1 hour until the chicken is tender. Taste and check seasoning before serving.

Serves 4

Curried Chicken Mayonnaise

An excellent way of serving cold chicken for an instant party dish.

Making time about 15 minutes

1 small onion, chopped
½ clove garlic, crushed
a little butter
1 tablespoon tomato purée
½ level teaspoon curry powder
1 tablespoon lemon juice
2 tablespoon apricot jam
½ pint (300 ml) good mayonnaise
12 oz (350 g) cooked chicken, diced
8 oz (225 g) cucumber, diced
2 oz (50 g) salted peanuts
small sprigs of watercress and lettuce to garnish

In a saucepan, gently sauté the onion with the garlic in the butter for 5 minutes or until soft. Add the tomato purée, curry powder, lemon juice and jam and heat gently until the jam has melted, then purée in a blender or sieve into a small bowl.

Cool, then add to the mayonnaise and mix well. Stir in the chicken and diced cucumber together with half of the peanuts.

Pile the chicken mixture onto a serving dish and surround with watercress, lettuce or more cucumber. Sprinkle the remaining peanuts over the top.

Serves 6

Fried Turkey Breasts

I like to serve turkey breasts very simply, cooked in butter with broccoli and sauté potatoes.

Preparation time about 5 minutes
Cooking time about 6 to 8 minutes

8 oz (225 g) turkey breasts
a little beaten egg
about 2 oz (50 g) fresh white breadcrumbs
about 2 oz (50 g) butter
lemon wedges

Place the turkey breasts between wetted greaseproof paper and beat flat with a rolling pin. The damp paper will stop the meat sticking to the rolling pin.

Dip the flattened turkey first in beaten egg and then into the breadcrumbs on a plate. Pat the breadcrumbs on firmly.

Heat the butter in a frying pan and fry the turkey for 3 to 4 minutes on each side until golden brown and crisp. The juices should run clear when a pointed knife is inserted in the centre. Lift out onto a serving dish and garnish with lemon wedges.

Serves 2 to 3

Manhatten Sweet and Sour Drumsticks

Cook the turkey drumsticks under a moderate grill to make them really tender.

Preparation time about 5 minutes
Cooking time about 20 minutes

1 tablespoon oil
1 tablespoon sherry
1 tablespoon soy sauce
1 teaspoon Worcestershire sauce
2 small turkey drumsticks

Heat the grill to moderate and remove the grill pan.

Blend the oil, sherry, soy sauce and Worcestershire sauce together and spoon over the drumsticks.

Place the drumsticks in the grill pan and pour over the baste and cook gently, turning and basting frequently, for about 20 minutes or until tender. Prod the thickest part of the drumstick with a skewer and if the juices run clear the meat is cooked.

Place the drumsticks on a serving dish and serve with savoury rice and a green salad.

Serves 2

Roast Turkey Florentine

Stuffing the turkey makes the meat go a little further, and it can also make a nice mid-week small roast.

Preparation time about 8 to 10 minutes
Cooking time about 45 minutes

1 lb (450 g) boneless turkey thigh
1 oz (25 g) butter
10½-oz (298-g) packet frozen cut leaf spinach

Stuffing
1 hard-boiled egg, chopped
2 oz (50 g) ham, chopped
2 oz (50 g) fresh white breadcrumbs
a little salt
freshly ground black pepper
1 egg, beaten

Heat the oven to 375°F, 190°C, gas mark 5.

Open the turkey thigh and lay it flat. Mix all the stuffing ingredients together and place in the centre of the meat. Roll the turkey around the stuffing and tie with string. Place in a roasting tin, spread with butter and then roast for about 45 minutes until tender.

Meanwhile, cook the spinach as directed on the packet.

Place the turkey on a serving dish and spoon the spinach around.

Serves 3 to 4

VEGETABLES

Vegetables come in infinite variety, and so do their uses in cookery. They can be a dish in their own right, part of a main dish, the basis of a nourishing soup, or they can be added to meat, fish or eggs. They give colour and flavour and they combine happily with each other. Potato, rice or pasta will make a small amount of meat go a long way. Fried potato turns a quick dish of bacon and eggs into a substantial meal.

Most vegetables need little preparation and they are best cooked quickly. Salad vegetables – lettuce, cucumber, spring onions, radishes, tomatoes – of course need no cooking at all and are a good accompaniment to supper dishes.

Use fresh vegetables when you can. Don't keep them too long but try to buy them as you need them. Choose those that are in season when they are cheapest and best.

Crisp Potato and Corn Fritters

Very quick to make, these fritters will make an ideal supper dish for the family to enjoy on a cold day. Serve them with bacon rashers, if liked.

Preparation time about 15 to 20 minutes
Cooking time about 8 minutes

1 lb (450 g) potatoes
1 large onion, grated
4 oz (100 g) sweetcorn, either canned or frozen cooked
2 eggs
salt and pepper
a little oil for frying

Cook the potatoes in their skins until only just tender, peel when cool enough to handle and then grate them on a coarse grater.

Mix together all the ingredients, except the oil.

Heat a little oil in a heavy frying pan. Drop the mixture in tablespoonfuls into the hot pan, then flatten with a fish slice and fry over a moderate heat for 8 minutes, turning once. You will be able to fry about 4 fritters at a time.

Lift out the fritters when golden brown on both sides, and keep them warm while frying the remaining mixture. This recipe will make about 12 fritters.

Serves 4

Potato Hot Pot

Serve this dish with oven-baked sausages or chops, and then all you will require is a green vegetable to complete the meal.

Preparation time about 15 minutes
Cooking time about 40 minutes

1 lb (450 g) potatoes, peeled and thinly sliced
8 oz (225 g) tomatoes, sliced
salt and pepper
1-oz (27-g) packet onion sauce mix
½ pint (300 ml) milk
4 oz (100 g) cheese, grated

Heat the oven to 425°F, 220°C, gas mark 7.

Arrange layers of potato and tomato slices in a shallow ovenproof dish, seasoning well between each layer.

Make up the sauce mix as directed on the packet, using the ½ pint (300 ml) milk, and pour over the vegetables. Sprinkle the cheese over the top and bake in the oven for 40 minutes until the potatoes are cooked and the cheese golden brown and bubbling.

Serves 4

Nutty Rice

This is an ideal dish for vegetarians.

Preparation time about 5 minutes
Cooking time about 45 minutes

> 5 tablespoons oil
> 1 green pepper, seeded and diced
> 1 onion, chopped
> 8 oz (225 g) brown rice
> 1 pint (600 ml) stock
> salt
> freshly ground black pepper
> 1 level teaspoon mixed herbs
> 4 oz (100 g) mushrooms, sliced
> 4 oz (100 g) cashew nuts, shelled
> 4 hard-boiled eggs
> chopped fresh chives

Heat the oil in a large saucepan, add the pepper and onion and cook for 5 minutes. Stir in the rice and cook gently until the oil is absorbed.

Add the stock, seasoning and herbs and bring back to the boil, then reduce the heat, cover the saucepan and simmer gently for 30 minutes, stirring occasionally. Stir in the mushrooms and continue cooking for a further 10 minutes or until the rice is tender and all the stock absorbed. Mix in the cashew nuts, and taste and check seasoning.

Pile the rice onto a warm serving dish. Quarter the eggs and arrange around the edge of the dish and sprinkle with chives. Serve immediately.

Serves 4

Simple Pizza

A scone mix makes a quick base for a pizza and cuts out on waiting for a bread dough to rise. Serve the pizza with a crisp green salad, tossed in French dressing.

Preparation time about 15 minutes
Cooking time about 25 minutes

6-oz (170-g) packet scone mix
milk
8-oz (227-g) can peeled tomatoes
1 onion, chopped
salt
freshly ground black pepper
1 level teaspoon mixed dried herbs
3 oz (75 g) Cheddar cheese, grated

Heat the oven to 425°F, 220°C, gas mark 7, and grease a baking tray.

Make up the scone mix as directed on the packet, using milk to give a soft dough. Roll out the dough on a lightly floured surface to make a circle 8 inches (20 cm) in diameter, and lift onto the baking tray.

Drain and chop the tomatoes and spread them over the scone base. Cover the tomatoes with the chopped onion, season well and then sprinkle over the herbs. Lastly, cover with the grated cheese and then bake in the oven for 25 minutes. When cooked the scone base should be a pale golden brown around the edge.

Serves 4

Cabbage Parcels

Nuts are used in the stuffing for these cabbage parcels, but you could use finely diced cooked bacon or ham. If you don't have any cooked rice, boil a good 2 oz (50 g) uncooked rice as directed on the packet.

Preparation time about 25 minutes
Cooking time about 30 minutes

> 1 tablespoon oil
> 4 sticks celery, chopped
> 4 oz (100 g) mixed unsalted nuts, chopped
> ½ teaspoon mixed herbs
> salt
> freshly ground black pepper
> ¼ pint (150 ml) stock
> 6 oz (175 g) cooked long grain rice
> 12 cabbage leaves
> 14-oz (397-g) can peeled tomatoes

Heat the oven to 350°F, 180°C, gas mark 4.

Heat the oil in a large saucepan and fry the celery for 5 minutes, then stir in the nuts, herbs, seasoning, stock and rice. Simmer gently, covered, until the stock has been absorbed, then taste and check seasoning.

Meanwhile, cook the cabbage leaves in boiling water for 2 minutes, then drain well and trim away the thickest part of the stalk.

Divide the rice mixture into 12 and place a portion in the centre of each leaf. Roll up each leaf firmly to form a parcel, tucking in the ends, and lay the parcels in a single layer in an ovenproof dish. Sieve the can of tomatoes, season well, and pour the purée over the cabbage parcels.

Bake in the oven for 30 minutes.

Serves 4

Potato Cheesies

Serve the cheesies straight from the frying pan with a fried egg and rashers of bacon to make an ideal high tea meal. If you have mashed potato left over this dish is a way of making the best of it next day.

Preparation time about 25 minutes
Cooking time about 6 minutes

8 oz (225 g) potatoes
1 tablespoon milk
4 oz (100 g) Cheddar cheese, grated
half an onion, finely chopped
1 tablespoon oil
salt
freshly ground black pepper
flour
1 egg, beaten
browned breadcrumbs
oil to fry

Peel the potatoes, cut them in quarters and cook in boiling salted water for about 10 minutes, or until tender. Drain and then mash the potatoes with the milk and add the cheese.

Fry the onion in the oil for about 5 minutes, until soft but not brown. Stir the onion into the potato mixture and season well.

Divide the mixture into 4 and shape into rounds, using a little flour. Coat each round in beaten egg and browned breadcrumbs.

Heat a little oil in a frying pan and fry the cheesies over a moderate heat for about 6 minutes until they are golden brown on both sides.

Serves 4

Crisp Corn Croquettes

These croquettes are coated in a packet of stuffing mix, which gives them a lovely crisp texture.

Preparation time about 25 minutes
Cooking time about 10 minutes

4 oz (100 g) frozen peas
1 large packet, 4½ oz (131 g), instant mashed potato
4 oz (100 g) cooked sweetcorn
1 tablespoon chopped parsley
salt and pepper
flour
1 egg, beaten
parsley and thyme stuffing mix
oil to fry

Cook the peas in boiling salted water for 5 minutes. Drain and roughly mash the peas to break them down a little.

Make up the instant mashed potato as directed on the packet, but using only ¾ pint (450 ml) boiling water. Stir in the peas, sweetcorn and parsley and season well.

Form the mixture into 8 croquettes, rolling them in the flour, then dip each in beaten egg and coat in the stuffing mix.

Fry in hot, shallow oil, turning frequently until golden brown and crisp. Lift the croquettes out of the oil and drain on kitchen paper. Serve hot.

Serves 4

Baked Tomatoes

Serve one tomato each for a first course, or serve two for a supper dish with buttered noodles tossed in plain yogurt and a crisp green salad. The Dutch beefsteak tomatoes are just the right size for baking and stuffing.

Preparation time about 10 minutes
Cooking time about 20 minutes

  6 large tomatoes
  2 oz (50 g) mushrooms, chopped
  2 oz (50 g) brown breadcrumbs
  ½ level teaspoon mixed dried herbs
  salt and pepper
  1 egg, beaten
  2 oz (50 g) cheese, grated
  a little oil

Heat the oven to 350°F, 180°C, gas mark 4, and lightly butter an ovenproof dish.

Cut a small slice from the top of each tomato and, using a teaspoon, carefully scoop out the insides of three of them and place the pulp in a bowl. Scoop out the insides of the other three and discard the pulp as it is not required for this recipe.

Add the mushrooms, breadcrumbs, herbs, seasoning and egg to the tomato pulp and mix well. Spoon this filling into the tomato cases, top with cheese and replace the lids. Brush the tomatoes with a little oil and place them in the ovenproof dish.

Cook in the oven for about 20 minutes.

Serves 3 or 6

Sweetcorn Soufflé Quiche

This quiche is a perfect dish to serve to vegetarian friends.

Preparation time about 5 minutes
Cooking time about 40 minutes

 14-oz (397-g) packet shortcrust pastry

Filling
  11½-oz (326-g) can sweetcorn
  just under ½ pint (300 ml) milk
  1 oz (25 g) butter
  1 oz (25 g) flour
  salt and pepper
  ½ level teaspoon paprika pepper
  2 eggs, separated
  2 oz (50 g) grated cheese

Heat the oven to 400°F, 200°C, gas mark 6, with a baking sheet in it. Roll out the pastry and line a 9-inch (22.5-cm) diameter deep metal flan tin. Prick well, then fill with a piece of crumpled greaseproof paper and baking beans. Bake blind for 10 minutes, then remove the paper and cook for a further 5 minutes to dry out the centre.

Meanwhile, drain the liquid from the sweetcorn and make it up to ½ pint (300 ml) with milk. Melt the butter in a saucepan, stir in the flour and cook for a minute. Blend in the milk mixture and bring to the boil, stirring until the sauce has thickened. Remove the pan from the heat and season well. Add the paprika pepper and beat in the egg yolks, together with the sweetcorn. Whisk the egg whites until stiff and then fold into the sauce. Turn the mixture into the flan and sprinkle with cheese.

Return the flan to the oven and reduce the heat to 375°F, 190°C, gas mark 5. Cook for about 25 minutes or until the quiche is set and well risen and a golden brown colour. Serve either hot or cold.

Serves 6

Ratatouille

Serve ratatouille with chunks of hot French bread and perhaps a bowl of freshly grated cheese.

Preparation time about 10 minutes
Cooking time about 25 to 30 minutes

1 green pepper
1 red pepper
3 tablespoons oil
2 medium-sized onions, sliced
4 courgettes, thinly sliced
12 oz (350 g) tomatoes
salt
freshly ground black pepper

Remove the seeds and pith from the green and red peppers and cut them into strips.

Heat the oil in a thick-bottomed saucepan, and add the peppers and onions. Cover and cook slowly for 15 minutes, stirring occasionally until the onions are soft.

Meanwhile, put the tomatoes in a bowl, cover with boiling water and leave to stand for 1 minute. Lift them out with a slotted spoon and remove the peel, then cut them in quarters and discard the seeds.

Add the tomatoes to the saucepan together with the courgettes and seasoning and cook, without the lid, for 10 to 15 minutes or until the courgettes are tender.

Taste and check seasoning and then turn into a warm serving dish.

Serves 4

Tomato and Vegetable Main Meal Soup

Make this filling soup when the larder is bare and you are hungry!
Serve with hunks of fresh bread and perhaps a finger or two of Cheddar cheese.

Preparation time about 5 minutes
Cooking time about 20 minutes

2 small onions
4 small carrots
1 potato
1½ oz (40 g) butter
1 oz (25 g) flour
1½ pints (900 ml) stock
5¼-oz (150-g) can tomato purée
salt and pepper
a little caster sugar
2 rounded tablespoons broken vermicelli
4 oz (100 g) cooked lean ham or bacon, cubed

Peel and very finely dice the onions, carrots and potato.

Melt the butter in a large saucepan, then add the vegetables and cook gently over a moderate heat for 10 minutes, without allowing the vegetables to colour.

Stir in the flour and cook for 1 minute. Gradually stir in the stock and the tomato purée and bring to the boil. Add seasoning, sugar and the vermicelli and simmer for about 6 minutes, by which time the pasta and the vegetables should be tender. Taste and check seasoning and serve very hot.

Serves 4

Spiced Stuffed Peppers

Adding anchovies to the rice stuffing for these peppers gives a tasty and unusual flavour to the dish. Serve with bread to soak up the juices.

Preparation time about 30 minutes
Cooking time about 30 to 35 minutes

4 large green peppers
1¾-oz (50-g) can anchovy fillets
1 large onion, chopped
1 clove garlic, crushed (optional)
4 oz (100 g) long grain rice
10½-oz (298-g) can condensed tomato soup
1½ soup cans of water
salt and pepper

Cut the tops off the peppers and scoop out the seeds and any white skin. Blanch the peppers in boiling water for 2 to 3 minutes, then plunge them into cold water to prevent further cooking.

Drain the oil from the anchovies into a small saucepan. Heat the oil, then add the onion and garlic, if used, and cook gently for 4 to 5 minutes without browning. Add the rice and continue cooking for 5 minutes, stirring all the time.

Add half of the can of soup and one full can of water to the saucepan, mix well and bring to the boil. Simmer very slowly, stirring occasionally, for about 15 minutes until all the liquid has been absorbed. Chop the anchovy fillets and add them to the rice. Season to taste.

Heat the oven to 375°F, 190°C, gas mark 5.

Fill the peppers with the stuffing and stand them in a small ovenproof dish. Mix the remaining soup and water together and pour a spoonful over the peppers and the rest around them. Put the tops back on the peppers, and then bake them in the oven for 30 to 35 minutes until tender.

Serves 4

Su's Plait

Nuts are used for the stuffing in this pastry plait instead of the usual sausage meat. They make a delicious filling, very moist and tasty.

Preparation time about 15 minutes
Cooking time about 30 minutes

14-oz (397-g) packet puff pastry
a little beaten egg or milk to glaze

Filling
4 oz (100 g) mixed unsalted nuts, chopped
1 onion, chopped
8-oz (227-g) can peeled tomatoes
1 teaspoon Worcestershire sauce
2 oz (50 g) mushrooms, chopped
1 oz (25 g) oatmeal
1 level teaspoon mixed dried herbs
salt
freshly ground black pepper

Heat the oven to 425°F, 220°C, gas mark 7.

Roll out the pastry on a lightly floured surface to an oblong 14 × 11 inches (35 × 27.5 cm).

Put the filling ingredients into a bowl and mix together thoroughly. Spread the mixture down the centre of the pastry. Make six diagonal cuts through the pastry about 2 inches (5 cm) apart to within 1 inch (2.5 cm) of the filling. Brush the edges of the pastry with a little beaten egg or milk and then alternatively wrap the pastry strips over the filling to form a plait.

Brush the plait all over with beaten egg or milk, lift onto a baking tray and bake in the oven for 30 minutes until golden brown.

Serves 4

French Bread Pizza

This is an ideal supper dish for hungry people – it is filling and full of flavour.

Preparation time about 15 minutes
Cooking time about 3 to 4 minutes

 2 tablespoons oil
 1 large onion, chopped
 1 clove garlic, crushed
 1 green pepper, chopped
 14-oz (397-g) can peeled tomatoes
 salt
 freshly ground black pepper
 4 oz (100 g) mushrooms, chopped
 a small French loaf or half a long stick
 4 oz (100 g) Cheddar cheese, grated

Heat the oil in a small saucepan and add the onion and garlic and fry for 3 to 4 minutes.

Add the green pepper and tomatoes and cook rapidly for about 10 minutes, stirring occasionally, until the mixture is thick and has reduced to about half the original quantity. Season well, add the mushrooms and cook for 1 minute.

Cut the bread in half horizontally and then cut each half across. Divide the mixture between the 4 pieces of bread.

Heat the grill to hot. Sprinkle the cheese over the tomato mixture and grill the pizzas until the cheese has melted and is golden brown and bubbly. Serve at once.

Serves 4

Pasta Creole

Serve this dish on its own with a bowl of freshly grated cheese or as an accompaniment to grilled sausages or chops.

Making time about 20 minutes

  6 oz (175 g) pasta noodles
  2 oz (50 g) butter
  1 onion, chopped
  1 green pepper, seeded and chopped
  1 red pepper, seeded and chopped
  8 oz (225 g) small courgettes, sliced
  8 oz (225 g) small tomatoes
  salt
  freshly ground black pepper

Cook the pasta noodles as directed on the packet and drain well.

Meanwhile, melt the butter in a large saucepan, add the onion and green and red peppers and fry for 3 to 4 minutes. Stir in the courgettes, cover the pan and cook for 12 minutes.

Put the tomatoes in a bowl, cover with boiling water and leave for 1 minute. Lift them out with a slotted spoon and skin them, then cut them into quarters and remove all the seeds. Add the tomatoes to the saucepan with the noodles and mix very thoroughly. Add salt and plenty of freshly ground black pepper to taste. Heat through until piping hot then turn into a warm serving dish.

Serves 4

Rumbledthumps

This is a variation on bubble and squeak. You could ring the changes by using kale or sprouts in place of cabbage.

Preparation time about 5 minutes
Cooking time about 20 minutes

1 lb (450 g) cooked mashed potato
1 lb (450 g) cooked shredded cabbage
1 rounded tablespoon chopped chives
salt
freshly ground black pepper
3 to 4 oz (75 to 100 g) Cheddar cheese, grated

Heat the oven to 400°F, 200°C, gas mark 6. Butter well a shallow ovenproof dish.

Mix together the potato, cabbage and chives and season well. Turn into the dish and sprinkle the top with cheese. Bake in the oven for about 20 minutes until the cheese has melted and browned and the vegetable mixture has heated through. Serve it as it is for a vegetarian meal, or with fried eggs or sausages.

Serves 4

Parsnip and Potato Cakes

This is an excellent way to use up left-over parsnips and mashed potato. The quantities are only approximate. Adjust them according to the amount of vegetables you have left over. Serve as an accompaniment to sausages or with fried eggs.

Preparation time about 10 minutes
Cooking time about 6 minutes

> *8 oz (225 g) cooked mashed potato*
> *8 oz (225 g) cooked mashed parsnips*
> *4 oz (100 g) cooked ham or bacon, finely chopped*
> *1 rounded tablespoon chopped parsley*
> *a little salt*
> *plenty of freshly ground black pepper*
> *about 3 oz (75 g) flour*
> *dripping to fry*

Combine the potato, parsnips, ham and parsley and then add seasoning to taste. Add sufficient flour to make a firm mixture. Mix well. Using well-floured hands shape the mixture into 8 rounds.

Heat the dripping in a frying pan and fry the cakes for about 3 minutes on each side until golden brown. Serve piping hot.

Serves 4

EGGS AND CHEESE

Eggs and cheese are blessed by all cooks. They are the great standby. With enough of them, and most households keep a good supply, the hostess is never at a loss for a quick meal, however unexpected her guests may be and however short a time she has to produce supper.

The two go together as though meant for each other and both combine with whatever vegetables are available. They marry happily with rice, pasta or potato. Children love them, vegetarian guests praise you for them and they satisfy the hungriest of husbands.

Keep a good supply of eggs and plenty of Cheddar and Parmesan cheese and you need never be at a loss for a quick supper dish.

Fried Sandwiches

I find that the children like to make these sandwiches themselves. The fillings may be varied to suit different people's tastes.

Preparation time about 10 minutes
Cooking time about 6 minutes

6 slices of white bread
4 oz (100 g) butter
3 slices of cheese or 3 slices of ham
salt and pepper
2 large eggs

Spread the bread with some of the butter and lay the cheese or ham on three of the slices and cover with the other slices, butterside innermost. Press the bread firmly together and trim off the crusts. Cut each sandwich into four squares.

Beat the seasoning and eggs together. Melt the remaining butter in a large frying pan. Dip each sandwich into the beaten egg and then fry in the butter over a moderate heat for 3 minutes on each side until crisp and golden brown.

Serve the sandwiches straight from the pan.

Serves 3

French Omelette

Omelette is the French word for a universally popular egg dish. Use a 6 to 7-inch (15 to 17.5-cm) omelette pan for a two to three egg omelette. The pan should have rounded sides and be of thick aluminium or cast iron. The new non stick ones make life easier. Never wash an omelette pan; wipe it out with clean kitchen paper and never use it for any other form of cookery.

Making time about 1 minute

3 eggs
3 teaspoons cold water
salt and pepper
½ oz (12.5 g) butter

Heat the omelette pan gently. Break the eggs into a bowl, add water and seasoning and beat lightly with a fork.

Put the butter in the pan and turn up the heat until the butter sizzles, but do not let it brown. Pour in the egg mixture.

With a fork or spatula, draw cooked egg from the edge of the pan inwards so that the liquid egg runs through to cook on the pan base. While the top is still slightly runny, fold over a third of the omelette away from the pan handle. Add any filling of your choice.

Grip the pan handle from underneath, with palm uppermost, and shake omelette to the edge of the pan away from the handle. Tip it over in three folds onto a warm serving dish.

Serves 1

Suggested fillings:

Grated cheese, sliced tomatoes, chopped cooked ham, sliced mushrooms cooked in a little butter, fresh chopped mixed herbs.

Spanish Omelette

This vegetable omelette is called *tortilla* in Spain and Mexico, *fritta* in Italy.

Making time about 12 minutes

1 tablespoon oil
4 oz (100 g) onion, chopped
1 green pepper, thinly sliced
1 tomato, sliced
4 oz (100 g) cooked diced potato
4 eggs
4 teaspoons cold water
salt and pepper

Heat the oil in an omelette pan. Add the onion and pepper and cook slowly for about 5 minutes until soft. Add the tomato and diced potato and heat through.

Heat the grill.

Prepare the omelette by beating the eggs, water and seasoning together with a fork. Pour into the hot onion mixture and cook, drawing the egg from the sides of the pan inwards so that the liquid egg runs through to cook on the pan base.

While the top is still slightly runny, place the pan under a hot grill until the top is just set.

Do not fold the omelette, slide it out flat.

Serves 2

Omelette Arnold Bennett

This dish is supposed to have been created especially for the famous writer by a chef from the Savoy hotel.

Making time about 10 minutes

  4 oz (100 g) smoked haddock, cooked and flaked
  2 oz (50 g) butter
  ¼ pint (150 ml) single cream, or less
  4 eggs, separated
  2 tablespoons Parmesan cheese, grated
  salt and pepper

Toss the haddock with half the butter and 2 tablespoons of cream in a thick pan over a quick heat, stirring well to mix. Remove from the heat and leave to cool.

Beat the egg yolks with half the cheese, salt and pepper. Add the fish mixture.

In a large bowl whisk the egg whites to form stiff peaks, then fold in the egg and fish mixture.

Melt the remaining butter in a large omelette pan over a moderate heat. Pour in the egg mixture and cook until the base is set and browned. Cover with the remaining cheese and cream. Place under the hot grill to brown quickly. Transfer to a warm dish and serve at once.

Serves 2

Pizza Omelette

This is far less filling than a traditional pizza and very much quicker to make.

Making time about 5 minutes

 6 eggs
 6 teaspoons cold water
 salt and pepper
 1 oz (25 g) butter
 1 level teaspoon mixed chopped fresh herbs
 1 level teaspoon tomato purée
 4 oz (100 g) ham, chopped
 2 tomatoes, skinned and sliced
 2 oz (50 g) sliced cheese

Beat the eggs with water and salt and pepper. Heat the grill to high.

Melt the butter in a large omelette pan, then increase the heat and pour in the egg mixture. With a fork or spatula draw the mixture from the sides to the middle of the pan, allowing the uncooked egg to set quickly. Repeat until all the egg is lightly cooked.

When the top is still runny, sprinkle on the herbs, then spread the tomato purée and ham over the omelette and arrange the tomato slices on top. Cover with cheese slices and place under a hot grill until the cheese melts.

Slide the omelette onto a warm serving dish and serve at once.

Serves 3

Chinese Omelette

This omelette needs only a salad and brown bread to make it a complete meal.

Making time about 7 minutes

1 oz (25 g) butter
1 small onion, very finely chopped
4 oz (100 g) bean sprouts, washed
2 oz (50 g) cooked ham, cut in very thin strips
4 eggs
1 tablespoon soy sauce
salt and pepper
2 spring onions, chopped

Melt the butter in an omelette pan over a moderate heat, add the onion, bean sprouts and ham and cook for 3 minutes, stirring occasionally.

Meanwhile, beat the eggs, soy sauce, salt and pepper together and heat the grill to high.

Pour the egg mixture into the omelette pan, and with a fork or spatula draw the mixture from the sides to the middle of the pan to allow the uncooked egg to set quickly. When the base of the omelette is set, place the pan under the grill until the top is lightly browned.

Slip the omelette onto a warm serving dish and sprinkle with spring onions. Serve at once.

Serves 2

Oven Fry

Sometimes I cook some button mushrooms, well seasoned in butter, in a dish in the oven at the same time as the bacon and I put a mound of them on top of each egg.

Preparation time about 3 minutes
Cooking time about 15 minutes

  ½ oz (12.5 g) butter
  8 rashers streaky bacon
  2 tomatoes
  4 eggs
  salt and pepper

Heat the oven to 400°F, 200°C, gas mark 6.

Butter four individual, shallow ovenproof dishes. Cut the rind from the bacon and put 2 rashers and a half tomato in each dish and bake in the oven for 10 minutes.

Crack an egg into the centre of each dish, return to the oven and bake for a further 5 minutes or until the egg is just set, the white should be firm and the yolk still soft. Season with salt and pepper and serve in the dishes in which they are cooked, with French bread or garlic rolls.

Serves 4

Gloucester Eggs

Serve this dish with noodles tossed in butter and fresh parsley. For four people you would need 8 oz (225 g) noodles.

Preparation time 12 minutes
Cooking time about 5 minutes

8 eggs
4 oz (100 g) double Gloucester cheese, grated
1 oz (25 g) butter
1 oz (25 g) flour
½ pint (300 ml) milk
½ level teaspoon made mustard
salt and pepper

Boil the eggs for only 8 minutes so that they are not completely hard, cool under running water and carefully remove the shells.

Make the cheese sauce (see Eggs Florentine, page 158), adding half the cheese.

Cut the eggs in half lengthwise and arrange cut side down in an oven-proof serving dish. Spoon the sauce over the eggs and sprinkle with the remaining cheese. Brown under a moderate grill for about 5 minutes, until golden brown and bubbling.

Serve with noodles and a green salad.

Serves 4

Egg and Vegetable Au Gratin

This makes an ideal vegetarian supper dish, and for those who are very hungry you could serve wholemeal bread or rolls.

Making time about 15 to 20 minutes

half a head of celery
1 cauliflower
6 hard-boiled eggs, halved
2 oz (50 g) butter
2 oz (50 g) flour
½ pint (300 ml) milk
salt
freshly ground black pepper
2 oz (50 g) fresh brown breadcrumbs
2 oz (50 g) grated Cheddar cheese
butter

Scrub the celery and cut into small chunks. Wash the cauliflower and break into florets. Place the prepared vegetables in a saucepan and barely cover them with boiling salted water. Simmer for 5 to 10 minutes or until the vegetables are just cooked. Drain well and reserve ½ pint (300 ml) of the cooking liquor. Turn the vegetables into a shallow ovenproof dish and arrange the eggs on top. Keep warm.

Melt the butter in a saucepan, stir in the flour and cook for 1 minute. Add the milk and vegetable cooking liquor and bring to the boil, stirring until thickened. Taste and add a little extra salt and plenty of freshly ground black pepper. Pour the sauce over the eggs and vegetables.

Heat the grill to hot.

Mix the breadcrumbs with the cheese and sprinkle over the top of the dish. Dot with a little extra butter and grill until the top is golden brown and crisp.

Serves 4

Curried Eggs

Serve with side dishes of mango chutney, sliced bananas tossed in lemon juice, poppadums and diced cucumber mixed with yogurt.

Preparation time about 15 minutes
Cooking time about 40 minutes

1 oz (25 g) margarine
1 onion, chopped
1 medium-sized cooking apple, peeled, cored and chopped
1 level tablespoon mild curry powder
2 oz (50 g) flour
1 level tablespoon soft brown sugar
1 pint (600 ml) chicken stock
juice of half a lemon
1 rounded tablespoon mango chutney
1 rounded teaspoon tomato purée
8 eggs
8 oz (225 g) long grain rice
salt
freshly ground black pepper

Melt the margarine in a saucepan, add the onion, cooking apple and curry powder and fry for 5 minutes, stirring occasionally. Blend in the flour and cook for 1 minute, then add the sugar, stock, lemon juice, chutney and tomato purée. Bring to the boil, stirring, then reduce the heat, cover the pan and simmer for 30 minutes.

Meanwhile, hard-boil the eggs for 10 minutes, and then plunge them into cold water. When cool, shell and dry the eggs on kitchen paper. Cook the rice in boiling salted water as directed on the packet, rinse and drain well. Keep warm.

To serve: put the eggs in the sauce and re-heat for 3 to 4 minutes, taste and season well. Place a border of rice around the edge of a serving dish and spoon the eggs and sauce into the centre.

Serves 4

Potato Egg Nests

This fast supper is ideal for children. If they are young one egg will be sufficient, but if a little older you will find that two eggs will usually disappear quite rapidly.

Preparation time about 5 minutes
Cooking time about 5 to 6 minutes

> butter
> 1 large packet, 4½ oz (131 g), instant mashed potato
> 1 pint (600 ml) boiling water
> 3 oz (75 g) Cheddar cheese, grated
> 4 eggs

Prepare a moderate grill. Butter well a large non-stick frying pan, about 10 inches (25 cm) in diameter.

Make up the mashed potato as directed on the packet, using the boiling water, and beat in 2 oz (50 g) of the Cheddar cheese.

Spread the potato in the frying pan and make four holes in it with the back of a spoon. Crack an egg into each hole and cook over a moderate heat for 2 to 3 minutes. Sprinkle over the remaining cheese and place under the grill for 3 to 4 minutes or until the whites have set and the yolks are still soft.

Serve at once straight from the pan.

Serves 2 or 4

Egg and Mushroom Supper Dish

This is a popular supper dish in our family, and good to serve to vegetarian friends.

Preparation time about 15 minutes
Cooking time 3 to 4 minutes

8 hard-boiled eggs
1½ oz (40 g) butter
4 oz (100 g) button mushrooms, sliced
1 green pepper, seeded and sliced
1½ oz (40 g) flour
¾ pint (450 ml) milk
1 tablespoon tomato ketchup
salt and pepper
2 oz (50 g) Cheddar cheese, grated

Butter a shallow ovenproof dish. Cut the eggs in half lengthwise and place cut side down in the dish.

Melt the butter in a small saucepan, stir in the mushrooms and pepper and cook over a gentle heat for 5 minutes. Add the flour and mix well. Cook for 1 minute, then blend in the milk and ketchup and bring to the boil, stirring until thickened. Simmer for 2 minutes, season well and then spoon over the eggs.

Heat the grill to moderate.

Sprinkle the dish with cheese and brown under the grill for 3 to 4 minutes or until the top is golden brown and bubbling.

Serve with plain boiled rice or noodles.

Serves 4

Eggs Florentine

Use either fresh or frozen leaf spinach. Adding a dash of nutmeg to the cheese sauce brings out the flavour.

Preparation time about 20 to 25 minutes
Cooking time about 5 minutes

> 1 lb (450 g) spinach
> 4 eggs
> ½ oz (12.5 g) butter
> salt and pepper

Cheese sauce
> 1 oz (25 g) butter
> 1 oz (25 g) flour
> ½ pint (300 ml) milk
> 3 oz (75 g) Cheddar cheese, grated
> salt
> freshly ground black pepper
> ¼ level teaspoon made mustard
> pinch nutmeg

Cook the spinach and drain well. Meanwhile, poach the eggs, remove from the heat and leave in the warm water.

Return the spinach to the pan, together with the butter and salt and pepper and stir over the heat for 1 minute. Arrange the spinach over the base of an ovenproof dish. Drain the eggs and place them on top.

Make the cheese sauce: melt the butter in a small saucepan, add the flour and cook for 1 minute, then stir in the milk and bring to the boil, stirring until the sauce has thickened. Stir in 2 oz (50 g) of the cheese together with the seasoning, mustard and nutmeg.

Spoon the sauce over the eggs and sprinkle with the remaining cheese, then brown under a hot grill for 4 to 5 minutes.

Serves 4

Cheese and Vegetable Soufflé

If you have any left-over cooked vegetables this soufflé makes a good economical supper dish. Use vegetables such as cauliflower, celery and carrots and make sure that they are crisply cooked.

Preparation time about 20 minutes
Cooking time about 40 minutes

 1½ oz (40 g) butter
 1½ oz (40 g) flour
 ½ pint (300 ml) hot milk
 salt and pepper
 1 level teaspoon made English mustard
 3 oz (75 g) Cheddar cheese, grated
 1 oz (25 g) Parmesan cheese, grated
 4 large eggs
 12 oz (350 g) crisply cooked vegetables

Heat the oven to 375°F, 190°C, gas mark 5 and place a thick baking sheet in it.

Melt the butter in a saucepan, stir in the flour and cook for 2 minutes. Remove the pan from the heat and stir in the hot milk, then return to the heat and bring to the boil, stirring until thickened. Add the seasoning and mustard. Turn the sauce into a large bowl to cool and stir in the cheese.

Separate the eggs and beat the yolks one at a time into the cheese sauce. Whisk the egg whites with a rotary hand or electric whisk until stiff but not dry. Stir 1 tablespoonful into the cheese sauce and then fold in the remainder carefully.

Butter a 2-pint (1-litre) soufflé dish and put the vegetables in the bottom. Pour in the cheese mixture. If you run a teaspoon around the edge this will make the soufflé rise evenly.

Bake the soufflé in the oven on the hot baking sheet for about 40 minutes until it is well risen and golden brown. Serve at once.

Serves 4

Flamenca Eggs

This is a Mexican dish. Serve it with chunks of French bread to make an ideal evening meal.

Making time about 25 minutes

  1 tablespoon oil
  2 large onions, sliced
  2 large tomatoes
  4 oz (100 g) bacon, chopped
  salt and pepper
  2 small canned red peppers, chopped
  4 eggs

Put the oil in a frying pan or heatproof serving dish, add the onions and fry gently for 10 minutes or until tender.

Meanwhile, put the tomatoes in a bowl, cover with boiling water and leave to stand for 1 minute. Remove with a slotted spoon and carefully peel off the skin and cut each tomato in slices.

Add the tomatoes and the bacon to the onion and cook for a further 10 minutes. Season well and stir in the red pepper.

Make four holes in the mixture in the frying pan and break an egg into each. Cook for 3 to 4 minutes or until the egg whites are set and the yolk still soft.

Serve at once from the dish in which it is cooked.

Serves 2 to 4

PUDDINGS

Puddings to round off your supper should be very simple. There is no need to spend time on elaborate preparation and guests will not welcome anything too rich or filling. Rely on fruit as much as you can – as a basis and as a flavour. Experiment with different mixtures – fresh oranges with raspberries, for example, or apricot and apple. Or you can make a few strawberries go a long way in a layer gâteau.

Serve ice cream with a difference, the difference being a home-made fruit sauce. You could make a variety of these sauces and keep them in the freezer for use as required.

On the other hand, you could always serve fresh fruit and cheese, and most of your guests will bless you.

Chocolate Coated Bananas

Chocolate coated bananas are rich and delicious, ideal for a special occasion. If you have a few spare minutes pipe the cream between the bananas to make them look even more tempting.

Making time about 8 minutes

3½-oz (100-g) bar plain chocolate
4 small bananas
¼ pint (150 ml) double cream, whipped

Break the chocolate into small pieces and place in a bowl over a pan of simmering water until melted.

Peel the bananas and cut them in half horizontally. Sandwich them together with whipped cream and place on a wire rack.

Spoon the chocolate over the bananas until the top is completely coated and a little has trickled down the sides. Leave in a cool place to set.

Serves 4

Honey Fruit Yogurt

If you make your own yogurt, here is a variation worth knowing – it needs no sugar.

Making time about 5 minutes

2 to 4 level tablespoons clear honey
½ pint (300 ml) natural yogurt
2 Cox's apples
2 oz (50 g) raisins, seedless

Blend the honey with the yogurt. Peel, quarter and core the apples, then slice and arrange in the bottom of four individual dishes and sprinkle over the raisins. Spoon the yogurt mixture on top. Chill well before serving.

Serves 4

Coffee Fudge Sundae

This is an easy-to-make sauce that adds a special touch to ice cream.

Making time about 5 minutes

> 3 oz (75 g) light soft brown sugar
> 1 oz (25 g) butter
> 1 level tablespoon instant coffee powder, or slightly less for a mild
>   flavour
> 2 tablespoons water
> 5 tablespoons evaporated milk
> 4 small bananas
> vanilla ice cream

Put the sugar, butter, coffee powder and water in a small saucepan and heat gently, stirring until the sugar has dissolved. Bring to the boil and cook for 1 minute, then remove from the heat and stir in the evaporated milk.

Slice the bananas into four individual glasses or dishes and spoon the ice cream on top. Pour over the hot sauce and serve at once with wafer biscuits.

Serves 4

Swiss Baked Alaska

This dish may be finished off while the meat plates are being cleared away. If the sponge base is ready before the meal starts, you only need to take the ice cream from the freezer and whip up the meringue for the topping.

Preparation time about 10 minutes
Cooking time about 3 minutes

1 small Swiss roll cut into 8 slices
a few Maraschino cherries
1 brick strawberry or vanilla ice cream

Meringue
3 egg whites
6 oz (175 g) caster sugar

Place the slices of Swiss roll close together on an ovenproof plate, then dot with a few Maraschino cherries and chill. Keep the ice cream very cold.

Make the meringue: whisk the egg whites with an electric or hand whisk until very stiff and then whisk in the sugar a teaspoonful at a time.

Heat the oven to 425°F, 220°C, gas mark 7, while eating the main course.

When the oven is up to temperature, place the ice cream on top of the Swiss roll and mask with the meringue, making sure that it is completely covered. Put in the oven for just 3 minutes so that the meringue is tinged a pale golden brown. Serve at once.

Serves 6

Chocolate Orange Flan

This is a delicious flan, very creamy and fattening. Serve it for a rather special meal.

Making time about 15 minutes
Chilling time about 1 hour

grated rind of 1 small orange
2 tablespoons orange juice
2-oz (50-g) bar plain chocolate
¼ pint (150 ml) double cream
1 sponge flan case
11-oz (312-g) can mandarin oranges

Place the orange rind and juice and the chocolate broken in small pieces in a small bowl and stand over a pan of gently simmering water until the chocolate has melted. Remove from the heat and leave to cool, but do not allow to set.

Whisk the cream until thick and then fold in the chocolate mixture.

Put the flan case on a serving dish. Drain the mandarins and place half in the sponge case, then cover with the chocolate cream. Finally arrange the remaining mandarins attractively on top of the chocolate and chill for 1 hour before serving.

Serves 4 to 6

Café Crème

So easy and so delicious!

Making time about 5 minutes

    ¼ pint (150 ml) whipping cream
    1½ to 2 tablespoons coffee essence
    15-oz (425-g) can Devon Custard
    a little grated chocolate

Whisk the cream with the coffee essence until it forms soft peaks, then fold in the custard.

Divide the mixture between three or four individual glasses or serving dishes and leave in a cool place until required.

Sprinkle with grated chocolate and serve.

Serves 3 to 4

Somerset Syllabub

Syllabubs are very quick and easy to make. If you have any white wine available it could be used in place of cider.

Making time about 5 minutes

½ pint (300 ml) double cream
grated rind and juice of 1 lemon
2 oz (50 g) caster sugar
6 to 8 tablespoons sweet cider

Place all the ingredients in a bowl and whisk with an electric or hand rotary whisk until the mixture is thick and will hold a soft peak. Taste and if necessary add a little extra sugar.

Divide between four individual glasses or serving dishes and serve with crisp biscuits.

Serves 4

Quick Chocolate Mousse

Very rich and filling but oh so nice!

Making time 10 minutes

  3½-oz (100-g) bar plain chocolate
  ½ oz (12.5 g) butter
  4 eggs

Break the chocolate into a basin and place over a saucepan half filled with gently simmering water. Stir occasionally until the chocolate has melted, then stir in the butter.

Separate the eggs and beat the yolks into the chocolate, then remove from the heat.

Whisk the egg whites until stiff, using an electric or hand rotary whisk. Fold into the chocolate mixture until evenly mixed using a metal spoon.

Divide the mixture between four glasses or individual serving dishes and leave in a cool place until required.

Serves 4

Pineapple Crush

This looks like a very special pudding, but it is really simple to make from ingredients that are usually in the store cupboard.

Preparation time about 10 minutes
Cooking time about 30 to 40 minutes

13¼-oz (376-g) can pineapple titbits
1 oz (25 g) cornflour
6 oz (175 g) caster sugar
2 eggs, separated

Heat the oven to 325°F, 160°C, gas mark 3.

Strain the juice from the can of pineapple and make up to ½ pint (300 ml) with water.

Put the cornflour in a small saucepan with 2 oz (50 g) caster sugar and stir in the pineapple liquid. Bring to the boil over a moderate heat, stirring until the sauce has thickened. Simmer for 1 minute. Beat in the egg yolks, with the pineapple and turn the mixture into a 2-pint (a good litre) ovenproof dish.

Whisk the egg whites until stiff and then whisk in the remaining sugar a teaspoonful at a time. Pile the meringue on top of the pineapple, spreading it out to the edges of the dish.

Bake in the oven for 30 to 40 minutes until the meringue is a pale golden brown all over. Serve at once.

Serves 4 to 6

Sticky Date and Orange Salad

There is no need to make a sugar syrup for this fruit salad. Layer the fruits with caster sugar the night before and leave it in the refrigerator to make its own syrup.

Making time about 15 minutes
Chilling time overnight

3 oranges
4 oz (100 g) whole dates
6 oz (175 g) seedless green grapes
6 oz (175 g) caster sugar
3 dessert apples
juice of 1 small lemon
2 oz (50 g) flaked almonds

Remove the peel and pith from the oranges and cut across into slices. Stone and chop the dates.

Put the oranges, dates and grapes into a serving bowl. Peel and core the apples, then cut into thin slices and add to the fruit with the caster sugar and lemon juice and stir lightly to mix.

Cover with a piece of foil and chill in the refrigerator overnight. Next day, sprinkle with nuts and serve with whipped cream.

Serves 4 to 6

Cheat Peach Condé

Canned rice pudding is beautifully creamy and adding egg yolks enriches the colour and makes the pudding more nutritious.

Preparation time about 5 minutes
Cooking time about 15 to 20 minutes

2 eggs, separated
15-oz (425-g) can creamed rice pudding
15-oz (425-g) can peach halves
3 oz (75 g) caster sugar

Stir the egg yolks into the creamed rice. Butter well an ovenproof serving dish and turn in the rice.

Heat the oven to 325°F, 160°C, gas mark 3.

Drain the peaches and arrange on the rice.

Whisk the egg whites until stiff and then gradually whisk in the sugar a teaspoonful at a time. Spoon over the peaches and rice, making sure that the meringue comes out to the sides of the dish.

Put in the oven for about 15 to 20 minutes until the meringue is tinged pale golden brown and the rice is hot through.

Serves 4

Fruit Fritters

Use apples, early rhubarb or bananas and serve at once with cream.

Preparation time about 10 minutes
Cooking time about 5 minutes

> 1 lb (450 g) rhubarb
> caster sugar
> 4 oz (100 g) plain flour
> 1 egg, separated
> ¼ pint (150 ml) milk
> oil for frying

Cut the rhubarb into 3-inch (7.5-cm) lengths, put on a plate and sprinkle with caster sugar.

Put the flour in a bowl and make a well in the centre, add the egg yolk and milk and blend to make a smooth batter. Whisk the egg white until stiff and then fold into the batter.

Heat the oil in a pan.

Dip the pieces of rhubarb into the batter one at a time and fry in the oil until golden brown. Lift out with a slotted spoon and drain on kitchen paper.

Serve at once with cream and sugar.

Serves 4

Apricot and Apple Crumble

Adding apricots to the ever-popular apple crumble gives it a great lift. If you forget to soak the apricots overnight, put them in a small saucepan, pour over boiling water and bring to the boil. Drain well. Alternatively, use a 15-oz (425-g) can of apricots, drained.

Preparation time overnight + 20 minutes
Cooking time about 40 to 45 minutes

4 oz (100 g) dried apricots
1 lb (450 g) cooking apples, weighed after peeling, coring and slicing
juice of half a lemon
3 oz (75 g) light soft brown sugar

Crumble
4 oz (100 g) plain flour
2 oz (50 g) caster sugar
2 oz (50 g) butter

Chop the apricots, place them in a bowl, cover with cold water and leave to soak overnight. Drain well.

Heat the oven to 400°F, 200°C, gas mark 6.

Put the apricots in a 2-pint (1.1-litre) ovenproof dish with the apples and lemon juice. Sprinkle brown sugar over the fruit and toss lightly to mix.

For the crumble: put the flour and sugar into a bowl and rub in the butter until the mixture resembles fine breadcrumbs. Sprinkle the crumble over the top of the fruit to cover.

Bake in the oven for 40 to 45 minutes until the crumble is brown and the fruit tender.

Serves 4 to 6

Butterscotch Bananas

Delicious – very rich and very bad for the figure! Butterscotch Bananas are lovely simply served on their own or with a little cream.

Making time about 6 minutes

1 oz (25 g) butter
4 small bananas
1½ oz (40 g) dark soft brown sugar
¼ level teaspoon cinnamon
6-oz (175-g) can evaporated milk

Melt the butter in a large frying pan. Halve the bananas lengthwise and then cut each piece in half.

Add the bananas to the pan and fry for 1 minute, then add the sugar, cinnamon and evaporated milk and shake the pan gently until the sugar has dissolved. Simmer for 3 minutes.

Serve at once allowing four pieces of banana for each portion.

Serves 4

Strawberry Layer Gâteau

This is a good way of making 8 oz (225 g) strawberries feed six – and of using up those that are different shapes and sizes.

Making time about 10 minutes

   ¼ pint (150 ml) whipping cream
   1 tablespoon vanilla sugar, or use caster sugar and add a little vanilla
     essence
   8 oz (225 g) strawberries
   1 oblong Madeira cake

Whisk the cream in a bowl until it is thick and will hold a soft peak, then whisk in the sugar. Put a quarter of the cream on one side for decoration.

Hull the strawberries, reserve 6 whole ones for decoration and then slice the remainder and fold into the large quantity of cream.

Cut the cake horizontally in three. Spread the base with half of the strawberry cream mixture, cover with the middle layer of sponge and then spread over the remaining strawberry mixture. Press the top of the cake on top of the cream.

Cover the cake with the plain cream and decorate with whole strawberries. If time allows, leave to chill in the refrigerator for about 1 hour.

Serves 6

Butterscotch Trifles

Make these trifles in individual serving dishes or glasses. This is a really quick pudding that is ready to eat within 15 minutes.

Making time about 10 minutes
Chilling time about 15 minutes

4 sponge trifle cakes
15-oz (425-g) can pear halves
1-pint (600-ml) packet butterscotch instant dessert mix
1 pint (600 ml) milk
4 walnut halves

Cut each sponge cake into six pieces and place in the bottom of four individual dishes.

Drain the pears, cut them in slices and divide between the dishes

Make up the instant dessert mix as directed on the packet and pour at once over the pears. Put in the refrigerator for about 15 minutes, then decorate with walnut halves and serve.

Serves 4

Apricot Delice

This pudding is made from ingredients usually found in the store cupboard; for a change use a can of raspberries with a raspberry jelly.

Making time about 45 minutes

1 lemon jelly
¼ pint (150 ml) boiling water
14-oz (397-g) can apricots
6-oz (175-g) can evaporated milk

Break up the jelly and dissolve in the boiling water. Strain the juice from the apricots and add to the jelly to make up to ¾ pint (450 ml), adding extra water if necessary. Put in a cool place until nearly set.

Purée the apricots in a blender until smooth. Whisk the evaporated milk with an electric whisk until really thick, then whisk in the jelly and fruit purée until the mixture is smooth and well blended.

Turn into a large bowl and leave to set.

Serves 6

Rosy Peach Macaroons

This is a delicious way to serve peaches.

Making time 20 minutes

4 peaches
½ pint (300 ml) water
4 oz (100 g) granulated sugar
2 level teaspoons arrowroot
cochineal
8 macaroons
¼ pint (150 ml) double cream

Halve the peaches and carefully remove the stones. Place the water and sugar in a shallow pan and heat gently until the sugar has dissolved. Place the peaches cut side down in the syrup and poach gently, turning them over once, for about 10 minutes or until they are cooked. The time will vary with the size of the peaches and you may find that 8 minutes is sufficient cooking time. Carefully lift out the peaches with a slotted spoon and peel off the skins.

Boil the syrup rapidly until reduced by at least half. Blend the arrowroot with a little cold water. Remove the pan from the heat and stir in the arrowroot, then return to the heat and bring back to the boil, stirring until the syrup is really thick. Add a few drops of cochineal to colour.

Place the macaroons on a serving dish and arrange a peach cut side down on each macaroon. Glaze each peach with the syrup.

Whisk the cream until thick and forms soft peaks and then pipe or spoon a blob on top of each peach.

Serves 4

Apple and Honey Snow

This is one of the best ways I know of using up windfall apples. Use the left-over egg yolks to make mayonnaise.

Making time about 30 minutes

1 lb (450 g) apples, weighed after preparation
knob of butter
2 thinly pared strips of orange or lemon rind
2 tablespoons thin honey
2 egg whites

Wash the apples, core and roughly chop. If you are using windfall apples, cut out any bruised pieces. Place the apples in a saucepan with the butter and orange or lemon rind, cover and cook over a very low heat for 10 to 15 minutes until soft. Remove the pan from the heat.

Put the honey in a bowl and then sieve the cooked apples on top. Stir well and leave to cool.

Whisk the egg whites until stiff and fold into the apple purée. Divide the mixture between four glasses and serve at once.

Serves 4

Pineapple Orange Fluff

This is a delicious pudding, quite good enough for a dinner party.

Making time about 20 minutes

15½-oz (439-g) can pineapple pieces or bits
grated rind and juice of 1 orange
2 eggs, separated
1 oz (25 g) cornflour
2 oz (50 g) caster sugar
glacé cherries

Drain the syrup from the pineapple into a measure, add the orange rind and juice and make up to ½ pint (300 ml) with water if necessary.

Put the egg yolks in a small saucepan with the cornflour and stir in a little of the syrup to make a smooth paste, then gradually stir in the remaining syrup. Cook over a moderate heat, stirring continually, until thick. Simmer for 1 minute, then remove from the heat and stir in the pineapple pieces. Leave to cool.

Whisk the egg white with an electric or hand whisk until stiff and then whisk in the caster sugar a teaspoonful at a time. Fold into the pineapple mixture and blend well.

Divide the mixture between four individual serving dishes or glasses. Decorate each with a glacé cherry and serve when required.

Serves 4

Hot Butterscotch Sauce

This simple sauce will turn ice cream into a special dish, and it's lovely served over slices of pineapple or banana.

Making time about 5 minutes

2 oz (50 g) butter
1 oz (25 g) light soft brown sugar
1 oz (25 g) dark soft brown sugar
2 level teaspoons cornflour
¼ pint (150 ml) milk

Put the butter and sugars in a small saucepan and heat gently until the butter has melted and the sugar dissolved. Remove the saucepan from the heat.

Blend the cornflour with the milk. Stir a little of the hot mixture from the saucepan onto the milk and then pour all the milk mixture into the pan.

Return the pan to the heat and bring to the boil, stirring until thickened. Simmer for 1 minute and serve the sauce hot.

Serves 4

Jiffy Fool

This is an ideal pudding to produce when unexpected friends pop in. Ring the changes and use any can of fruit you may have in the store cupboard.

Making time about 5 minutes

   15-oz (425-g) can peach slices, drained
   15-oz (425-g) can Devon custard

Purée the peaches in the blender and then gradually pour in the custard until mixed.

Turn the fool into a glass serving dish and leave in a cool place until required.

Serves 4

Mandarin Cream Gâteau

No need to use mandarins for this recipe, it can be made with any can of fruit from the store cupboard, but the juice should measure ¼ pint (150 ml).

Making time about 10 minutes

1 dairy cream sponge
11-oz (312-g) can mandarin oranges
4 level teaspoons cornflour

Lift the top layer of sponge off the cake and cut into six wedges.

Drain the juice from the mandarin oranges. Place the cornflour in a small saucepan and blend in the juice. Bring to the boil over a moderate heat, stirring until thickened. Simmer for 1 minute. Remove from the heat and stir in the mandarins. Leave to cool for 1 or 2 minutes, then pile back onto the cake.

Put the sponge sections back on top so that they point upwards showing the mound of fruit in the centre.

Keep the gâteau in a cool place until required.

Serves 6

Raspberry Creams

This recipe could be made with small whole wild strawberries instead of raspberries.

Making time about 10 minutes

1 egg white
2 level tablespoons caster sugar
grated rind and juice of half a lemon
¼ pint (150 ml) single cream
¼ pint (150 ml) double cream
8 to 12 oz (225 to 350 g) raspberries

Whisk the egg white until stiff and then whisk in the caster sugar, a teaspoonful at a time, until the mixture is like soft meringue.

Put the lemon rind in a bowl with the creams and whisk together until the cream will hold a soft peak. Whisk in the lemon juice.

Fold the meringue and raspberries into the cream, taste and add more sugar or lemon juice if necessary. Spoon into individual glasses.

Keep the creams in a cool place until required. Serve with crisp biscuits such as shortbread.

Serves 4

Apple Slice

It is not always easy to buy strudel pastry and I find that rolling out puff pastry very thinly gives a similar effect.

Preparation time about 15 minutes
Cooking time about 45 minutes

  14-oz (397-g) packet puff pastry
  1 lb (450 g) cooking apples
  2 oz (50 g) caster sugar
  ¼ level teaspoon cinnamon
  4 oz (100 g) currants
  milk

Heat the oven to 400°F, 200°C, gas mark 6.

Roll out the pastry very thinly on a lightly floured table to about 12 × 24 inches (30 × 60 cm).

Peel, core and slice the apples onto the pastry and arrange in lines. Mix together the sugar, cinnamon and currants and sprinkle over the apples.

Roll up the pastry from the narrow end. Place on a baking tray and brush with a little milk. Bake in the oven for 45 minutes, when the pastry will be golden brown and crisp and the apples tender.

Transfer the apple slice to a serving dish and serve warm with single cream or vanilla ice cream.

Serves 6

Fresh Oranges with Raspberries

Quick to make, this dessert stretches the first punnet of the new season's raspberries.

Making time about 10 minutes

    4 small oranges
    3 teaspoons caster sugar, or to taste
    small punnet of raspberries

Remove the peel and pith from the oranges and slice horizontally. Remove the pips. Reassemble the slices in the shape of the oranges and place in a glass serving dish.

Sprinkle with caster sugar and toss in a few raspberries. If time permits, chill in the refrigerator before serving.

Serves 4

Index